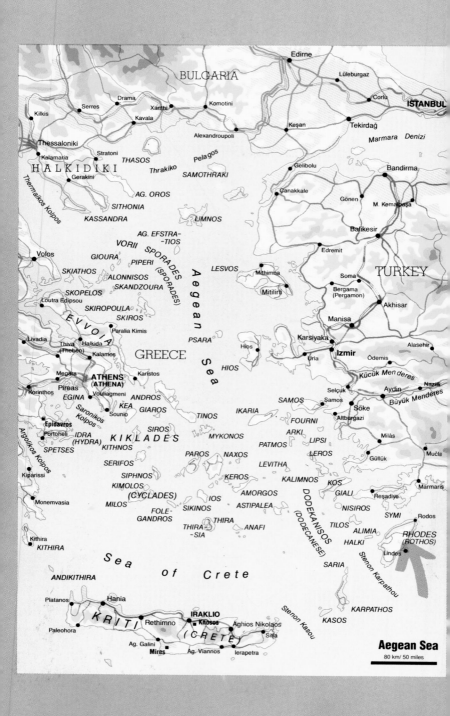

Aegean Sea
80 km/ 50 miles

RHODES

Paradisi

APA PUBLICATIONS

Welcome!

Byzantine monasteries, Crusader citadels, colourful fishing harbours, Greek hospitality...Rhodes, the sunniest and largest island of the Dodecanese, has plenty to attract visitors. Some come for its dune-backed sands and cosy tavernas where views of the Mediterranean come *gratis*; others to discover a fascinating history forged by Crusaders, Greeks and Ottomans in the old quarters of Rhodes Town and in picturesque Lindos. Whatever your own tastes, this guide shows you how to get the most out of this justly popular destination.

In the following pages Insight Guides' correspondent on Rhodes has created a selection of itineraries grouped around the island's four key bases: Rhodes City, Archangelos, Lindos and Gennadion. Designed to suit a variety of tastes and time frames, they include all the favourite sights but also many hidden gems that only someone intimately acquainted with Rhodes is likely to know – quiet beaches, remote monasteries and semi-wild archaeological sites. One of the author's aims has been to show how visitors can genuinely come into contact with the land and its people.

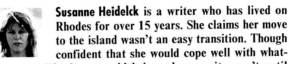 **Susanne Heidelck** is a writer who has lived on Rhodes for over 15 years. She claims her move to the island wasn't an easy transition. Though confident that she would cope well with whatever life there would bring, she says it wasn't until she began to love both the island and its people that she felt anything like equal to the task. To this day she frequently feels like an honoured guest who receives more from her hosts than she will ever be able to give.

C O N T E N T S

Pages 2/3: twilight over the port of Rhodes City

Lindos

Gennadion

Pages 8/9: fishing boat bow

A History of Foreign Occupation

'In answer to our query about which had been the best of all the
occupying powers, up to the present day, the old salt scratched his
head and replied that, actually, there had not been any great dif-
ferences between them. The main thing was to be occupied, spared
from independence, which would only bring higher taxes.'

from *The Seasick Whale* by Ephraim Kishon

There is scarcely a more laconic commentary on the history of
much-occupied Rhodes than that of the fisherman netted by Israeli
humorist Ephraim Kishon. Of course, Rhodes has long been and
remains subject to foreign occupation, whether by Turkish Janissaries,
who held the fortress walls for three centuries, Italian fascists, who
propelled the island into World War II or, indeed, by the
present-day hordes who roam the narrow alleyways of the Old Town in revealing

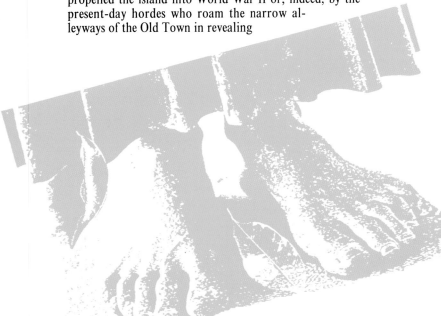

Culture

shorts and halter tops – the 'uniform' of the latest conquerors. It is indicative of the specifically Rhodian mentality that the locals have adjusted to even this latest, and perhaps most insidious, invasion. From the Ottoman turban to the German helmet, from the leather loincloth to the rattling suit of knightly armour, the inhabitants of this island have, of course, seen everything.

The sun-drenched silhouette of the capital city stands as an impressive testament to its oft changed cast of foreign masters. With its minarets, cupolas and church steeples, its imposing Palace of the Grand Masters and mighty, fortified ramparts, Rhodes City displays its history on its skyline. All this is outshone, however – and shone down upon – by the one to whom this island has always owed its first allegiance: the sun-god, Helios.

Of course, what dry modern science has surmised, the Greeks have known for centuries. It was Helios who brought the island to his father Zeus's attention when it suddenly popped up during the first tertiary period. As a result, he received the island as a gift and, in gratitude, decided to shower Rhodes with sunshine in perpetuity. The consequences of this particular 'occupation' were abundant harvests, wealth and a booming economy.

In antiquity, the island of Rhodes was a bustling trade centre with business connections throughout the entire Mediterranean region. Wine, wheat and oil found international markets as export goods, and great trading houses from Mesopotamia to Egypt maintained agencies in the city of Lindos, which at that time experienced a renaissance of cultural and economic growth. 'Ten Rhodians, ten ships,' was the saying. In other words, whoever lived on Rhodes was automatically considered a wealthy man.

The inhabitants of the island probably owed their wealth as much to the fact that they didn't go around senselessly swinging their swords as they did to the blessings of Helios. Skilled diplomats from the outset, they understood how to maintain what was a precarious but at any rate largely independent perch between the big power blocs of the day. In times of crisis, they actually allowed themselves to be occupied and then made the best of it. Only if the conditions set by the conquerors seemed exceedingly harsh would they defend themselves tooth and nail. Uncharacteristically, perhaps, they participated in the Trojan War. Apparently, it represented an opportunity to gain prestige.

In 408BC, the three extremely rich municipalities of Kamiros, Ialyssos and Lindos decided to found a city whose location would provide the best possible guarantee against encroachment from the east: Rhodes City. A street grid was designed according to the most modern architectural standards of the time which, in its rectilinear structure, is still visible today. Rhodes City rapidly consolidated its position as capital city and spiritual and economic centre of the island. Cicero, Caesar and Tiberius were students at its famous School of Rhetoric; ships from East and West passed through its harbour. An immense number of statues were erected to adorn the new metropolis, the inhabitants of which still numbered some 100,000 at the turn of the millennium – a population density which has never again been matched.

However, from the date of unification with Rome – seen from today's vantage as a great tactical error – the gradual decline of the city began. The island was incorporated as a Roman province of the rising power. Now, Rhodes provided its wine at a ridiculously low price to supply the disdainful and decadent imperial court, and was forced to make large deliveries. Furthermore, earthquakes constantly shook the land and epidemics reduced the population, weakening the island's defences towards the growing danger from the East. In AD515 Rhodes City was completely destroyed by an earthquake. The city built after the cataclysm corresponded in size to the Old Town of today. Drawn into the Byzantine Empire, Rhodes had to defend itself repeatedly through the centuries against the advancing charges of the Persians and Saracens. Many of the events of that period are shrouded in darkness. The curtain rises again in the year 1082, when two new occupying powers appeared on the busy Mediterranean stage: Venice and Genoa.

It was thanks to the Genoans that Rhodes fell into the hands of the Crusaders. In some fierce horse trading, a Genoan admiral (in reality a pirate), bartered away the entire island to the knights, who proceeded to make Rhodes their base for the next two centuries. For the purposes of the holy wars, and as the last strategic staging point before Con-

stantinople, Rhodes had all sorts of strategic advantages. What started out as an offensive campaign against the Turks soon degenerated into a war of defence, which is reflected in the increasingly impregnable fortifications which the knights erected on the island over the years.

But, neither cannons nor double walls were finally able to stop the inexorable approach of the Ottomans. Some 70 years after the sack of Constantinople, Rhodes City fell. On 22 December 1522, the Grand Master, Villiers de l'Isle Adam, had to capitulate with scarcely 200 men remaining to him. Sultan Suleiman I promised him and his people an honourable departure, and the majority of Rhodes' Greek population followed the departing Crusaders into exile. Remaining Rhodians who had fought alongside the knights were slaughtered, while others capitulated. They looked on as Christian churches were turned into mosques, and accepted the taxes which were levied to finance the Turkish administration. Since they

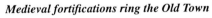

Medieval fortifications ring the Old Town

View over the roofs of the Old Town

were forbidden to set foot inside the capital after sunset, they settled outside the walls. On the ground plan of the ancient, spaciously planned city, the present day city, with its tangled network of streets, was overlaid.

By and large, the indigenous population adjusted well to the rule of the crescent. It wasn't until the 19th century that the Turks' hold on the island began to slip, as all over Greece rebellions rose up against the ruling dynasty. The Ottomans' response was reactionary. From 1874 on, they clamped down on trade, suspended religious freedom, and resorted to violent means in order to quell revolt. However, the course of history could not be altered and, by 1912, the Turks had been deposed by the Italians.

Once more the face of the island's capital underwent substantial alterations. Huge and pompous neoclassical buildings, which bring to mind the Via Nationali in Rome, sprang up. But though in the years 1922 to 1943, and particularly during the Fascist era, large tracts of land were expropriated, the Italians did much for the development of the island. Donkey paths were paved and the Palace of the Grand Masters, destroyed in an explosion, was reconstructed. Even today, a marble plaque still hangs there, paying homage to Benito Mussolini. Much was restored and renovated during the Italian occupation, although it could be said that it was not beautified nor, strictly speaking, preserved. Rhodes, viewed by the Italians as a vacation home for Axis dignitaries, can still look back with pride to many of the achievements of that time.

After the surrender of the Italians to the Allied forces in 1943, Rhodes became the site of many bitter battles which led at last to the final capitulation of the Germans in 1945. Up to the year 1947, the island remained under the command of the British, who restored order to the chaotic administrative apparatus. In 1948, Rhodes became part of Greece.

14

Historical Highlights

4000BC First human settlements on the island.

2500 Settlement by the Minoans.

1600 Rhodes' Mycenaean Period; settled by the Achaians, who found Lindos, Kamiros and Ialyssos.

1200 The Trojan War.

1100 Beginning of the Dorian migration. The Dorians divide the island into three areas with capitals in Lindos, Kamiros and Ialyssos.

1000–700 Formation of the six-city Dodecanese league, Hexapolis.

650 First Rhodian colonies on Sicily, Italy, Spain and France.

490 First Persian War. Rhodes is compelled to fight for the Persians. Greek victory at Marathon.

480 Second Persian War. Greek victory in the Battle of Salamis.

478 Rhodes joins Delian League.

408 Founding of the new capital, Rhodes City. Period of cultural and economic ascendancy.

336 Alexander the Great of Macedonia occupies Kos. Rhodes joins him against Persia.

331 Alexandria is founded. It becomes a vital trading partner.

323 Alexander's generals divide the conquered areas, leading to war. Rhodes allies with Egypt.

305 The Macedonian, Demetrios Poliorketes, lays siege to Rhodes for a year without success. The Colossus of Rhodes, a 34-m (111-ft 6in) bronze statue, is erected.

304 Rhodes establishes first relations with Rome.

227 Earthquake. The Colossus is demolished.

201 Philip of Macedonia occupies Rhodian possessions in Asia Minor. Rhodes asks Rome for help.

190 Rhodes joins Rome against Hannibal. Victory for Rome.

164 Alliance pact with Rome.

42 Cassius completely destroys the City of Rhodes and the fleet.

AD50 The apostle Paul lands at Lindos.

395 Rhodes becomes a province of the Eastern Roman Empire.

1125 Venice conquers Rhodes.

1306 Crusaders acquire Rhodes from a Genoan pirate. Great works – hospitals, fortifications – by the Knights of St John.

1457–1522 Failed Turkish attempts to take over the city.

1522 Six-month siege by Turkey under Suleiman the Magnificent.

1523 The Knights of St John capitulate. Rhodes remains under Turkish hegemony until 1912.

1912 Rhodes occupied by Italy.

1943 The German Wehrmacht invades Rhodes.

1945 British and Greek commandos liberate Rhodes.

1948 Treaty ratified and Rhodes and Dodecanese become part of Greek state, 7 March, 1948.

1949 Greek Civil War between Communists and US-backed Government forces comes to an end.

1967 Coup by the right-wing Colonels leads to dictatorship under the Junta.

1974 Democracy restored after Junta falls over Cyprus troubles.

1981 First socialist government, PASOK, elected.

1983 Greece joins the EU.

1988 UNESCO declares the City of Rhodes a World Heritage Site.

1990 PASOK loses elections to the Conservatives, Nea Demokratia.

1993 Rhodes celebrates the 2,400 year anniversary of the founding of Rhodos; PASOK re-elected.

1995 The 16 Mediterranean members of the World Tourism Organisation meet on Rhodes.

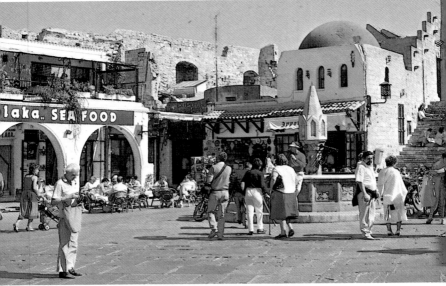

Hippokrates Square in the Old Town

Beaches and Watermelons

With a surface area of 1,412km² (545 square miles), Rhodes is the largest of the Dodecanese archipelago which, despite its name (*thótheka* means 12), consists of 14 islands. Only 18km (11 nautical miles) from the Turkish coast, Rhodes is the easternmost island in Europe, with the exception of the islet of Kastellorizo. From a geological point of view, the island should be considered part of the Turkish Taurus Massif. However, since 1948, Rhodes has been part of Greece, and Turkish speaking residents represent a small minority of the population. In addition to Greek, many elderly and even middle-aged Greeks speak Italian, which was the *lingua franca* during the occupation.

The distance from Cape Koumbourno – located on the 'nose' of the island, northeast of Rhodes City – down to Cape Prassonissi in the extreme southwest is 80km (50 miles). The island has an average width of some 28km (17 miles). The 220km (137 miles) of coastline consist, for the most part, of sand and gravel beaches on the east coast; half beach, half rock in the west.

The tallest mountain peaks are, in the west, the 900m (2,953ft) high Profitis Ilias and the all but barren 1,215m (3986ft) high Attaviros; and in the east, the 825m (2,707ft) Akramitis.

The heavy forestation of Rhodes in comparison to other Greek islands is a result of the relatively high amount of rainfall it receives, mainly between November and April. The increasing cultivation of watermelons on the island uses up a large portion of the water available to communities, so there are occasional water shortages in the villages, especially after drier winters. However, the north coast, with its large hotel complexes, remains largely unaffected.

There is a stark contrast between the north – overloaded with hotels, restaurants and other businesses – and the south which is less accessible to tourists and therefore largely orientated towards agriculture. Eighty percent of the commercial activity of the population is concentrated on only 10km^2 (4 square miles) of the island's surface area. Of the remaining area, approximately 17 percent is farmland; 32 percent pasture.

Foreign Exchange and Expensive Cigarettes

The history of Rhodes, which consists of an almost unbroken chain of foreign occupations, has made it easier for the populace to adjust to the modern variation on an old theme: tourism. Tourism has represented the main source of income on the island since the 1960s. Those farsighted enough to invest their money in land at that time were able to buy entire tracts of coast in the northwest of the island for a song. The high, not always well controlled credit policies of the Karamanlis government created, in 1966, the basis for a secure source of foreign exchange, from which the State received up to 25 percent profit. Because of its continually negative balance of trade, the Greek government cannot eschew this source of income.

Ninety percent of the tourism on the island consists of package tourism. Individual tourism does not even enter the economic equation. The prices for these package tours have remained relatively stable, since the annual rate of inflation (23–25 percent) is largely absorbed by the currency exchange rates. However, Greece's neighbour, and antagonist, Turkey, which is still a cheap country in which to travel, has become a serious competitor. In order to stop the charter tourists from wandering off to its more reasonably priced neighbour, Greece stipulates that such visitors may lose their return flights if they venture into Turkey for longer than 24 hours.

Thirty years ago, Rhodian farmers were able not only to feed the residents of their own island, but to export produce to the mainland and abroad. Today, fruit, vegetables, fish and meat must be imported. The capacity of the island to absorb more tourists expands unflaggingly. But the tourist balloon cannot be inflated indefinitely. There are already signs of a declining number of visitors, leading to empty hotel beds and bankruptcies.

The broad range of EU wares now available even in the villages has been accompanied by price increases which poorer island residents cannot afford. Because of increased tobacco taxes, status symbols such as foreign cigarettes are no longer within the reach of this segment of the population. However, since the island gives the traveller the impression of prosperity, it can be difficult to grasp fully the insecurity of the majority of Rhodes' residents.

Rhodes (Ródhos)

2 km / 1.25 miles

Aegean Sea

Rhodes City
Cape Zonari
Cape Vodi
Thermes
Kalithea
Kalithea
FALIRAKI BEACH
Cape Ladiko
Kritika
Rodini
Asgourou
Koskinou
Ixia
Tris
Trianda
Filerimos
Pastida
M. Eleoussa
Kalithies
PSALIDA
Cape Vagia
AFANDOU
Afandou
Kremasti
PARADISSI
Paradissi
Damatria
Mantsa
KOUMOULI
Loutani
Kolimbia
Moni Tsambika
TSAMBIKA
Cape Archangelos
Stegna
Theologos
Tholos
Epano Kalamonas
Petaloudes
Psinthos
Psinthos
Archangelos
PROFITIS ILIAS
M. Kalopetra
PSINTHOS
Spilia
MESSOVOUNA
Archipolis
Platanero
Soroni
Plati
Pikaria
Eleoussa
Epta Piges
Malona
Makka
Fanes
Agros
Dimilia
Platania
M. Ag. Nikolaos Fountoukli
Kalavarda
Salakos
Apollona
M. Artamiti
ASSOURI
Ancient Kamiros
Kapi
PROFITIS ILIAS
Cape Minas
Mirtonas
Nani
Embonas
Mandrikon
Attaviros
1215
ATTAVIROS
Kamiros Skala
Kritinia
Gilfada Bay
Kritinia Castle
AMARTOS
MAKRI
STRONGILO ISLAND
ALIMNIA ISLAND
Cape Pounenti
TRAGOUSSA ISLAND

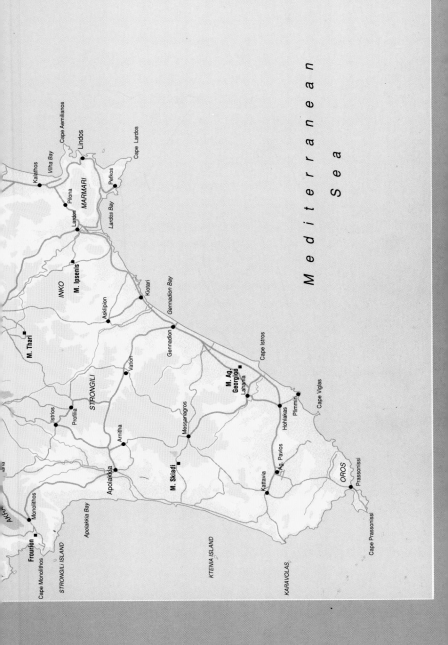

_M e d i t e r r a n e a n_

_S e a_

Cape Aemilianos

Lindos

Vliha Bay

Kalathos

Pilona

MARMARI

Cape Lardos

Perkos

Lardos

Lardos Bay

INKO

M. Ipsenis

Gennadion Bay

Kiotari

Askilpion

M. Thari

Gennadion

Vation

STRONGILI

Cape Istros

M. Ag.

Georgiou

Laharnia

Istros

Profilia

Messanagros

Amitha

Plimmiri

Cape Viglas

Hohlakas

Apolakkia

M. Skiadi

Ag. Pavlos

STRONGILI ISLAND

Monolithos

Apolakkia Bay

Kattavia

OROS

Prassonissi

Fraurion

Cape Monolithos

KTENIA ISLAND

KARAVOLAS

Cape Prassonissi

Rhodes City

Historical Rodos

Rhodes City *(Rodos)* is the most recent urban settlement on the island. In contrast to ancient Lindos, Kamiros and Ialyssos, the date of its construction can be pinpointed. In the year 408BC, the three older communities decided to found a city, the architectural plan of which was based on the theories held by the philosopher Hippodamos. The clear and distinctive road system; the well located port at the extreme northern tip of the island; the Acropolis, the amphitheatre and the stadium all became within a short time after construction the showplace of a significant culture. Rhodes City rose steadily in stature to become the island capital. In active cultural and economic exchange with Alexandria, the new Egyptian metropolis founded by Alexander the Great, a university came into being here, the library of which overshadowed even the world famous library of Alexandria. Education-hungry students from both the Orient and Occident, among them a large number of Roman emperors, came to study at ancient Rhodes.

However, the strategically desirable location did not bring growth, development and status without responsibility. Over the course of the subsequent turbulent centuries, it was the City of Rhodes which held out against attacks from the East.

The Palace of the Grand Masters

Rhodes City Today

Every year, millions of tourists flood through the narrow alleyways of the Old Town to visit the churches, museums and fortress walls, and familiarise themselves with the 2,400-year history of the island's capital. The surviving rich cultural mix etched graphically on the city's skyline from minarets to battlements, and the huge choice of holiday activities make Rhodes an appealing destination for a wide range of visitors. During the day you can follow in the footsteps of the Knights of St John, admire Mycenaean archaeological finds, and visit modern art galleries. After dark, quaint tavernas and bars await you in the Old Town squares, while music bars, discos and pubs enliven the New Town. You can see theatre and dance events in the new Melina Mercouri Theatre in the Medieval Moat, enjoy concerts from some of Greece's famous singing stars, learn Greek dancing at the Nelly Dimoglou Theatre or simply play a game of *távli* (Greek backgammon) with locals in a quiet *kafeneíon*.

Over the course of the last 30 years, the city has accommodated the demands of package tourists with several thousand hotel beds. But not all the big new hotels are bland and impersonal, as is sometimes supposed. In the New Town and along the east and west coasts there is a selection of luxury and middle-level accommodation for discerning visitors. For example, the new Rodos Imperial, one of the most expensive hotels in Greece, is one of the island's finest at Ixia. Most of the new hotels have tennis courts and swimming pools, and all rooms are air-conditioned. (Note: independent travellers will have difficulties finding a room in these hotels during high season.)

Alternatively, if you have a romantic side, you may like to rent one of the small pensions within the walls of the Old Town. In this price category, you cannot expect luxury, but in its place you will find a room with a special view. Just after dawn, when other tourists are still asleep in their hotel-palaces outside the walls, your own first glimpse out of the window will probably include a graceful palm tree, the cupola of a mosque, a plaza shaded by a huge plane tree or a peaceful interior courtyard resplendent with fuchsia, bougainvillaea and scented oleander. Before the shops open on **Sokratous Street (Odos Sokratous)**, and the facades are obstructed by stridently coloured souvenirs, you may still experience a moment of timeless Rhodes in one of the little plazas hidden away in the Old Town.

A Walk through the Old Town

Day tour: breakfast on Dorieos Square; Ibrahim Pasha Mosque; Square of Jewish Martyrs; lunch at the Plaka on Hippokrates Square; Greek coffee in a Turkish kafeneíon; a visit to a Turkish bath; Suleiman Mosque and Turkish Library; Palace of the Grand Masters; the Street of the Knights.

It is astonishing what an attraction tourists exert upon one another. They seem to congregate in the same places at the same times in order, it seems, just to remain together. One of the most obvious examples of this instinct can be observed on **Odos Sokratous (Othós Sokrátous)**, the main thoroughfare of the Old Town. As though part of a wave, they proceed up the hill; once at the top they swing off toward the **Palace of the Grand Masters**. While passing by they make a quick raid on the **Suleiman Mosque**, and then blend back into the crowd at the visitors' centre, returning to **Hippokrates Square** via the **Street of the Knights**. Naturally, individualists such as ourselves will put this busy tourist street behind us later on. However, first we can content ourselves with breakfast at the **Oasis Restaurant**, which is situated in one of the most beautiful squares of the Old Town, **Dorieos**.

In the early morning – English breakfast is served from 9am – it is pleasantly tranquil here, and thanks to a gigantic plane tree, it's also shady the whole day through. The square houses one of the most important mosques in the Old Town, the striking **Mosque of Redjeb Pasha**, built in 1588 and featuring a fountain made from Byzantine and medieval church columns. It contains the sarcophagus of the Pasha and is set in peaceful gardens.

In the surrounding alleys are small handicraft shops, cobblers, furriers and tailors' shops which have retained their authentic identities. The **Ibrahim Pasha Mosque** on nearby Sofokleous St, built in 1531 and refurbished in 1928, has an exquisite interior and is the city's oldest Islamic house of worship. If the door is open, take a look inside. It is recommended that men wear long trousers if they enter the mosque. The misleading pile of wooden sandals outside the entrance does *not* imply that you should use them: here bare feet are obligatory.

With the help of the map in the wallet at the back of this guide, or the excellent new 3D map of the Old Town by designer Mario Camerini (available at most tourist shops and restaurants), push on through to the **Square of the Jewish Martyrs, Plateia Evreon Martiron**.

The Palace of the Masters

The perplexing hodge-podge of alleys, dead ends, nooks and crannies in the medieval city contrasts sharply with the logical layout of the new quarter. However, it is still evident on the ground that in antiquity both sections of the city formed an integrated whole: **Odos Omirou** (Omiros Street); **Odos Agiou Fanariou** (St Fanourios Street); and **Odos Ippoton** (the Street of the Knights), still run along the original grid of the ancient city designed 2,400 years ago by the geometrician Hippodamus of Miletus.

We should now have reached the Square of the Jewish Martyrs by way of Pythagora Street. The square, with its little sea horse fountains and shady plane trees, was once the centre of Evriaki, the Jewish Quarter. On Rhodes, Jews made up a significant community, whose position remained unthreatened even during the era of Italian fascism. Tragically, the invasion of the island by the German Wehrmacht initiated a systematic extermination of the congregation's membership, which once numbered 2,000. Only 35 of the primarily Sephardic Jews managed to survive. On the entrance gate of the synagogue, which is hidden on a side street, **Dossiadou**, you will find a plaque which names the numerous victims of the Holocaust. Those who are interested in further exploring the more recent history of the Old Town should walk from Plateia Evreon

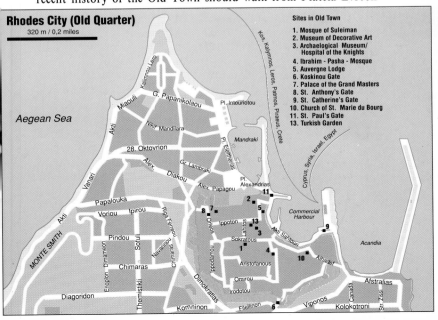

Rhodes City (Old Quarter)

320 m / 0,2 miles

Aegean Sea

Sites in Old Town

1. Mosque of Suleiman
2. Museum of Decorative Art
3. Archaeological Museum/ Hospital of the Knights
4. Ibrahim - Pasha - Mosque
5. Auvergne Lodge
6. Koskinou Gate
7. Palace of the Grand Masters
8. St. Anthony's Gate
9. St. Catherine's Gate
10. Church of St. Marie du Bourg
11. St. Paul's Gate
13. Turkish Garden

Martiron to Pindarou where the majority of the houses are of postwar construction. In this area, the Holocaust extended not only to the people, but also to their homes.

Of course, the walls of the city hold much more than the memories of these recent atrocities. The picturesque capital of Rhodes has been coveted by a string of ruthless conquerors for centuries, and what today appears to be the harmonious integration of a diverse variety of architectural styles and cultural elements is really the result of a chain of bloody wars and bitter defeats. Thus, the mosques were originally Crusader churches, which were purged of every representation of the human figure and then topped with minarets. Prior to this most recent transformation, however, the Knights of St John had 'renovated' Greek Orthodox churches, changing them into Roman Catholic cathedrals. One example is **Panagia tou Kastro, Our Lady of the Castle**, in Alexander the Great Square, which now houses the collection of Byzantine art.

We continue through **Aristotelous Street** to **Hippokrates Square**, a focal point for tourist traffic. Here you can sit very comfortably, for a somewhat inflated price, and enjoy a view of the former civil courthouse, the Kastellania, which now houses the library and Historical and Folklore Archive. Among the fish restaurants on the square, Plaka is one of the most popular, but fish, especially red snapper or barbouni is expensive.

In the Old Town

The afternoon tourist traffic on **Sokratous Street** should be pretty dense by now. Most of the things for sale are tacky odds and ends. Here you will also find (as in the new city) furriers touting their wares even in high summer, when bikinis would surely draw more buyers. Despite its overall character, just before the street forks you will find one of the most beautiful cafés (*kafeneía*) in the city, which is managed by a Turkish couple. Here the local men still drink their traditionally prepared Greek coffee and play *távli,* Greek backgammon, a close cousin of its Western counterpart. The distinctive clatter of the tiles is one of the unforgettable sounds of a Mediterranean summer.

After pausing for air and caffeine, plunge back into the crowd and turn left into Ag Fanourios, one of the medieval quarter's oldest and most famous streets, narrow, lit with wall lanterns and braced with flying arches to protect the houses during earthquakes. In a bid to bring peace to the Old Town it is officially a pedestrian precinct and traffic is banned by day apart from residents' vehicles, delivery vans and taxis. But motorcycles still cause a problem at night and many taxi drivers refuse to go in through the more tortuous gates such as the Koskinou Gate for fear of damaging their vehicles in the narrow lanes.

Leaving Ag Fanourios, you come to **Plateia Arionos** where you might like to sample the refurbished Turkish **steam baths of Mustafa Pasha**. Considered the finest in the east when they were built in 1558, the chambers are elaborately decorated and still fuelled by olive wood stoves. The huge dome-roofed main room with its ornamentation and marble floors is used only by men, while auxiliary rooms are reserved for women. Steam baths, masseurs (and masseuses) and an atmosphere of otherworldly calm make a visit to the baths an unusual experience. They are open from 7am–7pm daily except Sunday and Monday; bring your own soap and towels.

Pavement cafés on Hippokrates Square

Located one block further on is an open air theatre where **folk dances** from all over Greece are presented nightly. **Nelly Dimoglou**, the leader of the dance troupe, has spared no pains in seeking out, documenting, and choreographing traditional dances, previously handed down only through 'oral' tradition. (Nelly Dimoglou Theatre, Andronikou St, open May to October, performances 9.20pm, except Saturday and Sunday; for further information, tel: 20157/29085). Continuing on **Ippodamou**, on which several hostels are located, proceed to the **Mosque of Suleiman the Magnificent**, which looks down along Sokratous Street. The main landmark, the rose-tinted Mosque, was built in 1522 to commemorate the Sultan's victory over the Knights and was rebuilt in 1808. Its superb, but unsafe, minaret had to be removed in 1989 and now the mighty mosque is crumbling and locked up. The **Islamic Libary of Ahment Havuz**, opposite, dates from 1793 and is an interesting place to visit with rare and valuable manuscripts including the chronicle of the siege of Rhodes from 1522, a collection of rare Arabic and Persian manuscripts and two priceless, illuminated 15th- and 16th-century Korans. These Korans were stolen five years ago, traced to London, recovered by the police and returned in 1994.

Next stop is the **Palace of the Grand Masters** on Plateia Kleovoulou, which dominates both the old and new towns. There are several rooms open to the public and two permanent exhibitions, **Medieval Rhodes**, and the **Rhodes 2,400 Years** archaeological exhibition. An excellent guide with room plans and illustrations is on sale.

The Palace, which was inhabited during the Knights' period by the Grand Master and his guards, was badly damaged when the town fell to the Turks in 1522, then destroyed after an ammunition explosion in 1856. It was reconstructed by the Italians (1936) as a summer home for Mussolini and Victor Emmanuel III, neither of whom ever used it. Inside, a marble staircase leads up to interlinking rooms featuring marvellous mosaics taken from Kos. (You can join a tour around the walls of the Old Town every Tuesday and Saturday at 2.45pm, starting at the palace entrance).

From the Palace we step out into the **Loggia of St John** where the Knights used to muster for action, originally linked to the Church of St John which was blown up when the arms cache was struck by lightning. Now end this tour by walking down the most famous street in the Knights' Quarter, **Odos Ippoton** (the Street of the Knights), lined by the Inns of the various Tongues or na-

Idyllic scene in the Old Town

tionalities, which were used as banqueting halls and lodgings for visitors, while the knights lived a monastic existence elsewhere. It's so well preserved you can almost hear the clatter of horseshoes on the cobbles. On the corner of the street is an interesting gift shop run by the Ministry of Culture selling replicas of statues and artefacts on show in the museum, all with certificates of authentication.

A Stroll through the New City

A half-day tour: breakfast in the New Market; walk via Eleftherias Street to the Mosque of Murad Reis; Turkish Cemetery; a swim and/or a visit to the Aquarium; Amerikis Street towards the city walls; a detour through the park, and stopping for a Greek coffee on Dimokritas Street.

The **Port of Rhodes** has been a reloading point for export goods for thousands of years and remains a duty free zone today. This will be our starting point for a walk through the new city. Before

Mandraki Harbour

setting out on **Odos Eleftherias** (Freedom Street), flanked by neo-classical structures, you may want to have coffee or something more substantial in the **Nea Agora**, or New Market, where people come from all over Rhodes and the neighbouring islands of Halki and Symi to buy essentials. The circular market hall is a lively, colourful place and the hub of the New Town, with fresh fruit and vegetable stalls, butcher's shops and bakers rubbing shoulders with stores specialising in nuts, gifts and duty-free drink. The market is full of little cafés and stalls selling everything from fresh orange juice to *souvlaki* and *gyro* with pitta-bread, the giant kebabs (*gyros*) of meat gently spit-roasting.

View of the Nea Agora (New Market)

As you stroll through the market you have to run the gauntlet of waiters trying to drum up trade for their restaurants. The vulnerable and hungry should choose with care: the pavement cafés overlooking the harbour tend to be pricey, but are pleasant spots to watch the world go by. The snack bars within the market are cheap and cheerful and used by the locals.

The fish market in the centre of all the bustle is in an elaborate domed building, elevated high above the action. The rest of the market is full of stalls selling costume jewellery, belts and T-shirts. Local shoppers use some of the little bars here as post restantes for parcels being sent to neighbouring islands and outlying villages.

In contrast to the new market, which has existed only since the turn of the century, **Odos Eleftherias** (Freedom Street), down which we now set off, sprang up during a yet later period of Italian building activity. It runs straight as an arrow out to the port and illustrates the Fascist era's love of monumental buildings (the present-day Bank of Greece and the main Post Office, for example).

On the right, as you proceed, you will see the fortifications which run around **Mandraki Harbour**, the furthest outpost of which — **Saint Nicholas Fort** — was intended to withstand the onslaughts

of the Ottoman Turks. According to legend, it was here that the famous **Colossus of Rhodes** was raised, though the precise placing of the great feet, has never been determined. The statue, erected in homage to the sun god, Helios, is alleged to have been some 34m (112ft) tall, but it fell in pieces during an earthquake only 65 years after its completion. For some seven centuries, the bronze wreckage is said to have lain before the walls of the city, until a Syrian Jew loaded it on to 900 camels and transported it to his home. (More sober scientific estimates have placed the number of camels at 90 at the most.) Nevertheless, the bronze giant was counted among the Seven Wonders of the World and has become, along with the windmills and the coy Rhodian deer, synonymous with Rhodes. Perched on pillars, a bronze stag and doe guard the entrance to the harbour at the point where the Colossus may have stood. Deer are the symbols of the city as they rid the island of snakes in antiquity. For years a herd of deer lived in the moat of the Old Town but now a sanctuary has been set up for them in Rhodini Park.

If you proceed straight ahead, behind the neo-Venetian Prefecture, you will run right into into the elegant minaret of the **Mosque of Murad Reis**, the admiral of Sultan Suleiman the Magnificent who was killed in battle in 1522. The mosque, built in his honour, fronts the Turkish cemetery where Islamic VIPs lie beneath elaborate Turban-shaped tombstones. The British writer Lawrence Durrell lived within the cemetery's precincts in the Villa Kleovoulos at the end of World War II. As the British press attaché, he had the thankless task of re-establishing Rhodes' press. His book, *Reflections on a Marine Venus,* contains a humorous description of these chaotic, postwar years, during which, for a brief time, the native population was subordinate to British officers.

A surprise awaits you when you step into the garden to the west of the Turkish Cemetery. Here stands the luxury hotel, **Des Roses**, constructed by the Italians in 1928. It has stood empty since the 1940s, but its dark and echoing room are set to come to life again when the city's casino moves here in the near future.

Those who have had enough of sightseeing might want to take this opportunity to head for **Elli beach** which begins behind **Plateia Kountourioutou**. Those still in search of further stimulation won't want to miss the **Aquarium** (open from 9am–4.30pm), at the most northern tip of the city. Besides the corals, sea horses and scorpions, you'll also encounter such stuffed curiosities here as a seven-legged calf, located on the upper storey.

The way back brings us down **Amerikis Street**, which leads directly into the Old Town. A visit to the park may be a welcome diversion. There is an attractive café on **Dimokratia Street** under cedar and plane trees, which is popular among high school students. Surrounded by their loud discussion, you can enjoy some more local colour before plunging back into the Old Town.

View of the Palace of the Grand Masters

A Full Day on the West Coast

Excursion from Rhodes City down the west coast road through Theologos, with its ruined Temple of Apollo, to Ancient Kamiros; Kritinia Castle; Kritinia, and its kafeneía; fish dinner in Kamiros Skala (or wine tasting and dinner in Embonas).

This car or motorcycle tour duplicates, for about a third of its route, the excursion outlined in Tour 4: *Through Paradissi to the Valley of the Butterflies.* However, today we will not be turning off for Paradissi but will, instead, continue in the direction of Kamiros. The terrain on the west coast is not as wild, steep and fissured as the south of the island, but the climate is fresher and usually gets the full force of the Meltemi wind.

The first historically significant site, which you will pass after about 20km (12 miles), is the village of **Theologos**, also called Tholos, where the remains of an ancient **Temple of Apollo** are found. Among the artefacts on the site is a marble tablet listing the names of priests, eloquent testimony to the former importance of the cult.

Approximately 3km (2 miles) past Kalavarda, an avenue of pines

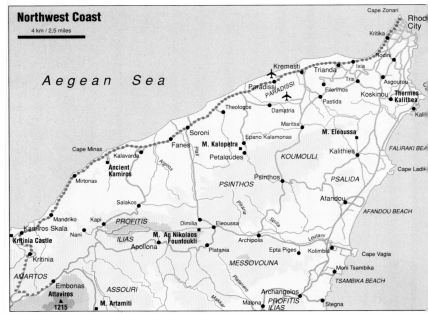

Northwest Coast

4 km / 2,5 miles

A e g e a n   S e a

Remains at Kamiros

on the left leads to the smallest settlement of the historic Dorian Three City League, **Ancient Kamiros** (open 8.30am–5pm, closed Monday). Kamiros, the flourishing but mysteriously abandoned Doric city discovered in 1859, is one of the west coast's major archaeological attractions. It was a thriving agricultural community during the 5th century BC and is now one of the best-preserved Classical Greek city sites.

The original ground-plan is exposed – you can even see the plumbing – along gently shelving terraces with stunning sea views west to Crete. Although named after the grandson of Helios, Kamiros was founded by Althaemenes of Crete and was probably destroyed in an earthquake in 142BC, although no-one is certain. The city lay forgotten for centuries until the British Consul Bilotti and French archaeologist Alzman began excavations where villagers had found ancient graves. The necropolis or cemetery yielded many 3rd-century BC treasures, several in the British Musuem and others, like the touching marble stele of Krito and her dead mother, in the Archaeological Museum in Rhodes Town.

The lay-out of the streets and houses is clearly defined, punctuated by the pillars of temples and topped by the remains of a great stoa. Sights include the remains of a 3rd-century BC Doric Temple, possibly of Pythian Apollo and altar to Helios; Hellenistic shops

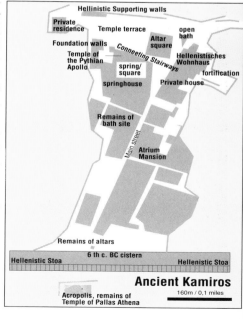

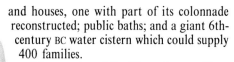

and houses, one with part of its colonnade reconstructed; public baths; and a giant 6th-century BC water cistern which could supply 400 families.

The remains of the 6th-century BC Temple of Athena Polias are on the top terrace, below which are vestiges of the once-magnificent Doric Stoa, 206m (640 ft) long. The area behind the stoa was the agora or market place, and to the left is a row of pits where treasures were stored. Unlike other sites on Rhodes, Kamiros was undisturbed by Byzantium, Christianity or the Knights. After a brief stop for refreshments at one of the tavernas on the coastal road below the site, head towards Kamiros Skala, the former port of Ancient Kamiros, with the ruins of **Kritinia Castle** perched on the crags above. Follow the signs to the castle, right up a gravel road through the farmland to the castle walls. Heavily fortified by the Knights of St John, the 15th-century ruins are perched above the sea with wonderful views to Halki, the deserted island of Alimnia and on a fine day down to Karpathos. Inland you can also see the white-washed village of Kritinia, founded by Cretan settlers. While clambering over the castle ruins take care – there is a sheer drop from the battlements.

Back at the main road again, a few kilometres further uphill is the turn-off for the village of **Kritinia**. A detour off the main road is worthwhile for the small Folk Museum located on the outskirts of the village, and in the centre are two *kafeneía* which have preserved their typical village character. These traditional Greek cafés are interesting for their attractive pink and turquoise colour schemes. Stroll through the village to see other traditional structures and architectural elements. Kritinia was founded by the son of a Cretan king. An oracle had prophesied that the son would kill his father and so the young man departed, and founded the village of Kritinia on Rhodes. He lived there peacefully until his aged father, near death and desirous of seeing his son one last time, sailed over from Crete. Unfortunately, his fleet was thought to be hostile, and the oracle's portent came true.

Now you must choose between two alternatives: free wine or great fish. **Embonas**, the main wine-producing area of Rhodes and home of the Emery winery, offers wine tastings to visitors (further information on Embonas is detailed in Tour 10). If fish appeals more than wine, head back to Kamiros Skala, the small fishing harbour and berth for ferries to Halki. There are three good fish restaurants, all popular at weekends (Kalamares is an excellent choice, but the furthest place, Taverna Loukas, is a favourite lunchtime haunt and meeting place for anyone heading to Halki). After an early meal, a dip in the wine-dark Aegean concludes your tour of the historical and gastronomic highlights of the west coast.

Through Paradissi to the Valley of the Butterflies

A half day trip from Rhodes City, via Paradissi, to the Valley of the Butterflies (Petaloúthes); Psinthos; Pastida; Maritsa; the Filerimos Plateau and Monastery; Ialyssos; Tris, and its tavérna.

Set out on this tour as early as possible, because you have a lot to cover in half a day. Naturally, you can lengthen your stay at the suggested stops and extend this tour into a whole day. But whatever you decide, you should take along good hiking shoes and some provisions. One more thing: if you ride, you'll have an opportunity to do so at **Mike's Horses**, in the area of Mount Filerimos (tel: 21387, open from 9am–1pm, and 4–8pm.)

Your route first takes you out of Rhodes City in a westerly direction towards Paradissi airport, passing many hotels and commercial buildings that have sprung up along this route. Villages such as **Kremasti** (famous for its festival for the Dormition of the Virgin Mary in August with stalls and fun-fair) and **Trianda**, which were lively communities of the **Ialyssos** region several thousand years ago, are today continuously expanding strips of package tour accomodation, their village centres obliterated by development.

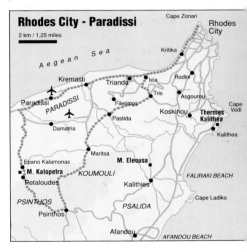

About 3km (2 miles) after Paradissi, turn left into the little road for **Kalamonas**. Proceed through the village. After about 2km (1 mile) you will arrive at the entrance to **Petaloudes,** the Valley of the Butterflies (which are really moths). The Jersey Tiger moths once gathered in their thousands for summer rest, attracted by the scent of oriental amber and sweet gum trees, but now their numbers have dwindled. The moths are dull brown at rest, but their wings flash scarlet when they fly, so few people can resist the temptation to set them in motion. Now signs ban clapping and any other noise likely to disturb them.

Of course, even without the fauna, a hike here is well worth your time. The path guides you through a surprisingly green vale lined

Restored monastery buildings at Filerimo

with unusual trees and punctuated by springs: do not drink from these springs, or even wash fruit in the water. Flowing through the middle of the 2km (1 mile) long gorge, is a brook easily crossed by wooden bridges. If you want to rest after your hike, you will find a cosy *tavérna* at the end of the valley.

We continue now on a relatively poor road through **Psinthos**, **Maritsa** and **Pastida** in the direction of **Mount Filermos**. Although not particularly attractive, Psinthos is historically important as the battle that was waged here on 17 May 1912 marked the end of the Turkish occupation.

A small detour takes you to a Byzantine chapel just outside Maritsa. Head left towards Kalaminas then about 300m (328yds) before the entrance to the village, and continue until you cross a bridge about 1km (⅝ mile) further on. Five hundred metres (547yds) to the left stands the late Byzantine church of **Aghios Nikolas Foundoukis**, which gets its name from the hazelnut trees that used to grow profusely in the area.

A remarkable detail on the interior frescoes are the eyes of the saints, all of which have been stabbed out. The Turks were not, as is commonly thought, responsible for this desecration. Instead, it is a manifestation of medieval superstition. At that time eye disorders were 'treated' by taking mortar from the eyes of holy frescoes, beating it into a powder and then mixing it into an infusion drunk by the patient.

From **Maritsa** proceed straight on to the centre of **Pastida**. Here a street sign points the way to Ialyssos. The asphalt, however, turns to gravel beyond the village. After a straight stretch of one or two kilometres, the road forks. The road to the right leads to the previously mentioned riding stables; the left fork goes up to the **Filerimos Plateau**, which lies 267m (876ft) above sea level. If you want to hike, tighten your laces at the first hairpin turn. Count on a good hour, longer in high summer. Because of the dense forest here, it is pleasantly cool in autumn and spring. The route now winds uphill through stands of fragrant pine and cypress. Lovely views of the Aegean Sea and beyond the City of Rhodes are worth the climb.

Filerimos translates as 'Friend of Solitude'. Byzantine era hermits, who erected a **monastery** here in the early Middle Ages, gave this name to the mountain. At the top you will see the remains of an old basilica next to the large car-park. However, first take some time to inspect the **monastery** grounds. The monastery itself is famous for its Calvary or Stations of the Cross, an avenue with monuments depicting Christ's Crucifixion which leads to a towering Crucifix where you can climb the internal stairs and look out over the plain.

As is usual on Rhodes, layers of ruins lie beneath other ruins. Thus, the baptistry, which still exists in fragments next to the renovated bell tower, was erected on the site of an ancient temple. Ialyssos, formerly 'Achaia', is supposed to have been settled two millennia before the arrival of the Achaians. Here on the summit, next to the monastery church, was the **Temple of Athena Poliados and Zeus Polieas**.

Those interested in a detailed art historian's survey of the Filerimos Plateau can obtain a special guide book from the kiosk by the monastery church. Also available here is a famed seven-herb liqueur called koleander, which is brewed by Italian monks and is supposed to benefit the digestive system.

Proceed downhill again in the direction of **Trianda**. At the last hairpin curve on the mountain, a sign points towards **Tris**, situated off the main Trianda road away from all the tourist development. This settlement, not even indicated on many maps, boasts one of the island's finest restaurants, **Ta Koupia** (also spelt Quipia). Now very popular with discerning, trendy Rhodians and international clientele, it specialises in refined Greek cuisine, and is located on the main street.

Map labels:
Temple of Athena Poliados and Zeus Polieas
Cloisters
Gallery
Knights' Church
Belfry
Spring
Early Christian Baptistry
Abbot's Residence

Filerimos
16 m / 0,01 miles

IALYSSOS

Ialyssos, in antiquity one of the three administrative regions of the island alongside Lindos and Kamiros, was essentially an agrarian community. There was no city of Ialyssos, *per se,* but only a loose linkage of communities which lay around the mountain. But the region, which in pre-Christian times administered the entire northern tip of the island, was unusually wealthy, as finds on the slopes of Filerimos have demonstrated.

The placement of Ialyssos' fortress – in an easterly direction from the monastery – was desirable from a strategic standpoint. From the peak, the entire northern end of the island can be surveyed. Whoever wished to conquer Rhodes had to conentrate their forces on Ialyssos and Mount Filerimos before they had any chance of conquering the rest of the island.

The Kallithea Hot Springs and Monte Smith

A half-day tour from Rhodes City to Thermei Kallithea, a Moorish baths complex; the lively resort of Faliraki; a climb up to the ancient Acropolis on Monte Smith; the day ends with a first-rate dinner at Vlachos Taverna.

This afternoon excursion south to **Faliraki** takes you out of town through urban landscapes dotted with industrial installations, docks, and repair shops and intersected by rather dull streets. The view remains the same beyond the city limits. Building cranes, excavated plots and half-finished hotel bunkers all amply illustrate how every metre of the northeastern coast is being exploited for the purposes of tourism.

After about 9km (6 miles), you will see a sign for the **Hot Springs of Kallithea**. This picturesque spa with its Moorish arches and domes was built by the Italians at the beginning of the century. To be sure, the mineral springs of Kallithea were already known in ancient times. The physician Hippocrates, who was born in 460BC on the island of Kos, extolled their beneficial effects on liver, kidney and rheumatic complaints.

Popular as a film set and recently used for an episode of *Poirot* on British TV, the spa has otherwise been disused since the end of World War II and as a consequence has a rather surreal feel with its crumbling facades. However, with a little imagination, one can resurrect the elegant international coterie in the mosque-like hall,

The Hot Springs at Kallithea

Thermei Kallithea, built by the Italians in the oriental style

come to 'take the waters'. The park alone, with its waving palms, pruned hedges, columns, and its continuously changing view of the Aegean, makes a longer expedition worthwhile. After viewing the buildings, take a dip in the sea at the little swimming cove below the springs.

Try to avoid the standard, rather dull fare on offer in most of the restaurants in **Faliraki**, which is 4km (2 miles) further south. This village, built solely for tourists, has some 200,000 beds available, including many belonging to Club 18–30. It has good nightlife, some of the island's finest beaches, and is connected to Rhodes by a regular bus service. From the gigantic water slide to the tennis courts, saunas, surfing and go-kart racing facilities, you can work out in style. Recent additions include an extensive shopping mall and bungee jump.

The return route leads back via the same road to the edge of Rhodes City. At the Supermarket Miko, located to the right just behind the city boundary sign, self-reliant (and self-catering) holiday-makers may want to stock up on reasonably priced European Community products, from Irish butter to Italian salami and German coffee. Particularly worth noting are reasonably priced Greek wines and international spirits. The supermarket's opening hours are posted at the entrance.

To reach your last stop, the ancient ruins atop **Monte Smith**, turn left behind the small bridge at the cemetery and drive straight on down Ana Marias Street, on the other side of the main road to Lindos. At the end of this track, turn right into Themistokli Sofouli Street until you reach Diagoridon, which branches to the left, leading you directly to the old stadium. However, be attentive. The direction of this one-way street changes frequently, and it is quite probable you will reach your goal after several detours.

If you park your car at the corner of Diagoridon and Themistokli Sofouli streets, you can combine your expedition through the ancient City of Rhodes with a half-hour-long hike up to the hill of Monte Smith, technically Agios Stephanos, but renamed after British Admiral Sir Sidney Smith kept watch for the Napoleonic Fleet from its heights. Even if you're not that interested in archaeology, it's worth the trip for the wonderful twilight panorama over Rhodes town to the Turkish coast.

As in many other places on Rhodes, Italian archaeological groups have tried their hand at restoring the ancient remains on Monte Smith. As a result, the complete reconstruction of the **stadium**, 200m (219yds) wide and 530m (580yds) long, as well as the small **amphitheatre**, with its marble staircases, provides a relatively vivid picture of the ancient Rhodian lifestyle. On the other hand, it takes a stretch of the imagination to conjure up an image of the glory that was once Rhodes City from the four remaining columns of the **Temple of Apollo** or the wreckage of the Acropolis.

Then, if you are too tired to face the descent on foot, catch the bus No 5 which plies, every 30mins, backwards and forwards between the Temple of Apollo and Mandraki. It will deposit you back where you started at the beginning of this itinerary. You can conclude your excursion with a first-rate Greek meal at the excellent **Vlachos Taverna**, tucked away on Mikhail Petrides Street near the Blue Sky Hotel.

Accommodation

Hotels in Rhodes are measured in six categories – luxury and "A" to "E". There are hotels of all categories up to A-class in most resorts and luxury hotels in Rhodes Town, Ixia, Faliraki and Kalathos. Rates vary between Low Season (October to May) and High Season (June to September).

Rooms in private homes can be rented at any time of the year.

LUXURY

RODOS PARK SUITES, Riga Ferou 12, tel: 24612
GRAND HOTEL, Akti Miaouli, tel: 26284
RODOS PALACE, Ixia, tel: 25222
RHODOS IMPERIAL, Ixia, tel: 75000
ESPEROS VILLAGE, Faliraki, tel: 85112
ATRIUM PALACE, Kalathos, tel: 0244 42345

"A"
RODOS BAY, Ixia, tel: 23661
ESPEROS PALACE, Faliraki, tel: 85734
CATHRIN, Ladiko Bay, tel: 85080

"B"
AGLAIA, A. Amerikis, tel: 22061
CONSTANTIN, Amerikis 65, tel: 22971
IRIS, Afandou, tel: 52233
ELEONAS APTS, Iaiysos, tel: 93791

SELECTED INEXPENSIVE HOTELS IN RHODES OLD AND NEW TOWN
PARIS, Ag. Fanouriou 88, tel: 26356
TEHERAN, Sofokleous 41B, tel: 27594
CASTRO, Arionos 14, tel: 20446
STELLA, Dilberaki 58, tel: 24935

Car and Bike Hire

EXPRESS RENT A CAR, Papanikolaou 17, tel: 24672
ALAMO RENT A CAR, Mandilara 64 and Airport, tel: 75970
J&D RENT A CAR, Faliraki, tel: 85885
MIKE'S RENT A MOTORBIKE, I. Kazouli 23, tel: 37420

Restaurants

Greek Specialities and Fish Restaurants

ALEXIS (FISH), Socratous 18, Old Town, tel: 29347, 35802. One of Greece's top 10 tavernas specialise in fish.
DINORIS (FISH), Museum Square, Old Town, tel: 25824. Reliable seafood.
ARGO (FISH), Haraki, tel: 0244 51410. Idyllic waterside taverna.
PALIA ISTORIA, Dendrinou 108, tel: 32421. Excellent. Qualiguide award.
SALT & PEPPER, M. Petridi 76, tel: 65494. *Mezes* and unique specialities.
TO STEKI, Asgourou, tel: 62182.
SANDY BEACH, Iaiysos Bay, tel: 94600.
ROMEO, Menekleous 7–9, Old Town, tel: 25186. Mezes, seafood, steaks, live music.
RUSTICO, Ippodamou 3–5, Old Town, tel: 23182. Mezes and more.

Chinese/Asian/ International Cuisine

QUEEN'S GARDEN, Valaoritou 1, tel: 35360. Good Szechuan cooking.
PAGODA, Faliraki, tel: 66287. Chinese specialities with Thai influence.
7.5 WONDER, Dilberaki 15, tel: 39805. Swedish chefs blend French, Mediterranean and Eastern classics.

British Cuisine

MOLLYE'S BRITISH DINER, I. Dragoumi 25, tel: 75328. Good value.
PARTNER'S BISTRO, Faliraki, tel: 85620. Best of British, huge portions.
LES ARCS BISTRO, Konstantopedeos 16. Inspired Anglo-French cooking with Greek elements.

Italian Cuisine

CLEO'S, Ag. Fanouriou 17, tel: 28415. Exquisite Italian-French cooking.
FELICIA, Griva 61. Low-priced pasta/pizza place.
LA CASA DI PASTA, Mandilara 28, tel: 75834. Good pasta.

Haute Cuisine

LA ROTISSERIE, Rodos Palace, Ixia, tel: 25222. Renowned chef, classic dishes.
MARCO POLO, Rhodos Imperial, Ixia, tel: 75000. Post-nouvelle Sino-Italian dishes prepared to perfection.
LE GOURMET, Ixia (opposite Miramare Hotel), tel: 90829. Good steaks.

Nightlife

In the Old Town, a deadly quiet descends, around midnight. By contrast, in the New Town, you can hardly move without walking into a bar.

Old Town

CAFÉ CHANTANT, Aristotelous 22. Boïte-style with loud, live Greek music.
ISLE FLOTTANTE, Sofokleous. Cheap hang-out for bohemian intellectuals.
ANCIENT MARKET GARDEN BAR, Omirou 70, tel: 34561. A boozer with a flavour of the Middle Ages.
NYN & AEL, tel: 35995. Hi-tech bar, medieval setting.

New Town

MINUIT, Kastelorizou (100 Palms Sq), tel: 34647. Music, dancing.
JUNGLE AT LE PALAIS, 25 March, tel: 32632. Best disco on Rhodes. Very popular. Cool off in adjacent lagoon.

BLUE LAGOON, 25 March, tel: 76072. Theme bar. Recreates set from *Hook*.
CHRISTOS GARDEN BAR, Griva 59, tel: 32144. Drinking oasis and art gallery.
SHIP INN, Dilberaki 34, tel: 37770. British-style pub with games.
STICKY FINGERS, A Zervou 6, tel: 35744. The original live rock music bar.

CAFE BROWN: 100, Palm Square. Sophisticated bar.
CASINO: currently in the Grand Hotel, tel: 28109. Smart casual dress required. Due to move to the former Rodon (Roses) Hotel in late 1996.

Theatres and Museums

The Sound and Light/Son et Lumière performs from April to October as follows: **Greek**: Sunday 9.15pm; **English**: Monday, Tuesday 8.15pm; Wednesday, Friday and Saturday 9.15pm; Thursday 10.15pm; **French**: Wednesday and Sunday 8.15pm; **German**: Friday and Saturday 8.15pm; Tuesday and Thursday 9.15pm; Wednesday 10.15pm; **Swedish**: Thursday 8.15pm; Monday 9.15pm; Tuesday and Saturday 10.15pm.
Information: Sound and Light Box Office, tel: 21922.

Nelly Dimoglou's Greek Folk Dances in the Old Town Theatre (behind the Turkish Baths). Telephone 20157 or 29085 for details.

Museums

ARCHAEOLOGICAL MUSEUM, Hospital of the Knights, Plateia Moussiou. Finds from the Mycenaean Period, and the Marine Venus, a 3rd-century BC Aphrodite. Tuesday to Sunday 8.30am–3pm, closed Monday.
BYZANTINE MUSEUM, Panagia tou Kastrou, Alexander the Great Square.
MUSEUM OF POPULAR ART, Plateia Argyrokastrou. Tuesday to Sunday 8.30am–3pm, closed Monday.
PALACE OF THE GRAND MASTERS, on Ippotron Street. Displays detail of the city in the Middle Ages as well as ancient finds, plus mosaics, notably the Nine Muses. Tuesday to Sunday 8.30am–3pm, closed Monday.
   Entrance to museums and archaeological sites is free on Sunday.

ARCHANGELOS

With its 3,300 residents, the town of **Archangelos (Arkángelos)** is the second largest settlement on the island. The name of the town refers to the Archangel Michael, to whom the main town church is dedicated. Archangelos is proud of its **ceramic industry** and **carpet 'factory'**, where you can order a carpet woven according to your own specifications. Traditional knee-high boots – originally worn to protect legs from snakes in the fields – can also be made to measure by local cobblers, but they don't come cheap. Made from sturdy cowhide and goatskin – snakes hate the smell of goats – the colourful boots can be worn on either foot. Located above the village are the ruins of a **Crusader fortress**, constructed by Grand Master Orsini in the year 1467 to provide protection against the Turks. **Stegna**, the closest beach, is 3km (2 miles) away and is therefore best reached by car or motorbike.

Archangelos and Environs

A full-day tour originating in Archangelos, where you can visit the potter Panagiotis; then proceed on to the Seven Springs (Eptá Pigés); and Kolimbia Beach for a swim and dinner; followed by an afternoon hike up to Tsambika Monastery.

It's not necessary to set out on this tour at the crack of dawn, since there are no great distances to cover. Have a big breakfast at one of the many breakfast bars on the main street in **Archangelos** and then take a quick look at the colourful woven rugs flapping in the breeze outside shops surrounding the bus stop. Folded, these carpets will fit into any suitcase and, at approximately £8–10, are reasonably priced souvenirs.

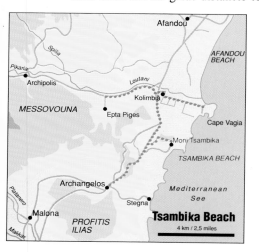

Tsambika Beach
4 km / 2,5 miles

Continue to the centre of the village, where the two main roads meet, and follow the signs by the bridge to **Stegna**. This road through the fields leads you to the top of a hill which has a fine view towards the sea. Here, turn left and, after roughly 500m (547yds), arrive at the cottage of the potter **Panagiotis**, whose kiln can be spotted just to the right on the edge of the path. As you enter his shady yard, you will probably find him sitting before his potter's wheel. Although he doesn't know you, he will almost certainly greet you as though you were an old friend and offer you an *oúzo*. This can be quietly sipped as you examine his assortment of ceramics. (Naturally, Panagiotis accepts commissions.) In addition to the **amphorae**, crafted according to ancient traditions, take a look at his unique wooden bed, intended for alfresco afternoon siestas and positioned at the edge of the cliff above the sea.

After visiting the potter, follow the road back through the fields and turn right into the main road to Rhodes Town, which leads steeply uphill. From here you can enjoy a good view of **Tsambika Bay** and, perched high above, Tsambika Monastery. Then proceeding down, take the left fork in the road in the direction of **Epta Piges/Archipolis**. After 3km (2 miles), take a sharp left turn in the middle of a right-hand curve and head uphill to **Seven Springs**

Inviting sea and sand: Kolimbia Beach

(Epta Piges), one of the island's lushest beauty spots nestling in the pinewoods. There's a car park and restaurant beneath the shady trees. A stream flows just below the restaurant, part of the irrigation system installed by the Italians to water the orange grove of **Kolimbia**. It is fed by the same seven springs which gave the place its name.

The entrance to a tunnel is located a metre or so from the restaurant and, at the end of the tunnel, the stream ends in a light green pool. Those not afraid to roll up their trousers and wade into the dark will be rewarded by what they find on the other side of the tunnel. However, the faint at heart can reach the place more easily by simply climbing the hill. In addition to the pool, you may want to photograph the colourful peacocks which live in the restaurant grounds.

After a rest and a cool drink in the shade, return to Kolimbia crossroads. Head over the main road down an arrow-straight avenue of eucalyptus trees in the direction of **Kolimbia Beach**. Here, it's up to you which way to turn when the road forks. In recent years, this whole area has become a prime destination for sun-seeking foreign tourists, and a series of new hotels and restaurants have sprung up to serve their needs. On Kolimbia's beautiful

beach, you will find loungers and umbrellas as well as facilities for water sports and boating excursions.

Leaving Kolimbia Beach, return to the main road, where after about 2km (1 mile) a turn left leads to **Tsambika Monastery**. Avid hikers should park their cars beyond the first hairpin turn. Others will want to creep a bit further up the mountain in first gear. The steep track ends at a seemingly interminable flight of steps rising through the pinewoods to the monastery, which is perched on the conical mountain peak. Childless women climb up to the chapel to pray to the miraculous icon of the Virgin Mary for help in conceiving. The 11th-century icon was found on the mountain by a childless couple, and the wife, believed barren, later conceived. If the pilgrims' prayers for motherhood are answered they pledge to name their children Tsambikos or Tsambika in gratitude – names that are unique to the island.

The splendid view from the summit, at 300m (984ft), takes in Faliraki to the northeast, Cape Lindos to the southwest and, to the west, the imposing Attaviros Massif.

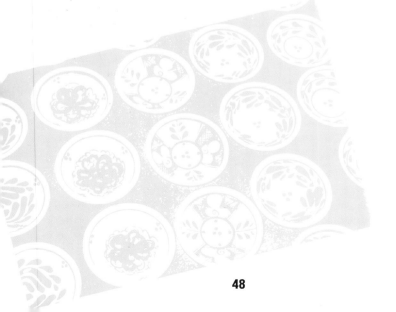

An Afternoon in Malóna and Haraki

An afternoon tour from Archangelos, via the old national road, to Malona and Haraki; then, a 1½ hour walk to Feraklos Castle. The day ends with a fish dinner at the Argo Restaurant.

Between 3 and 4pm, leave Archangelos wearing good walking shoes, and head south following signs for the Old National Road posted

Haraki's beach promenade and the fortress of Feraklos

at the intersection on the main street. After 6km (4 miles) you will reach **Malóna,** and the so-called fruit basket of Rhodes. This fertile valley is the site of Rhodes' largest orange grove. The **oranges,** which are harvested twice a year (end of May and end of October), are outstanding as juice oranges, so purchase a kilo of *portokália* in Malona.

Another gourmet attraction in Malona is the village bakery. Here you will find the best bread on Rhodes, baked in traditional wood fired ovens. The fragrant, sour dough loaves may be bought hot from the oven between 3 and 4pm on weekdays. For those new to the area, the bakery, used mainly by local people, may be a little difficult to find – Malóna, and the neighbouring village of Massari, are still wholly intact Greek villages which have not succumbed to the tourism rampant at the beach settlement of Haraki. To avoid

49

Fish tavérna in Haraki

getting lost, stop just before you reach the little bridge on the village road, and ask a passerby for directions to the bakery: *Pou íneh o foúrnos?*

Now double back to the traffic lights at the entrance to the village where, a couple of metres to the right, you reach the main road for Lindos/Rhodes Town. Beyond the intersection, the road leads straight ahead to **Haraki**, whose special charm lies in the graceful, Italian promenade stretching all the way around the port. Here you will find – a rarity on Rhodes – many Greek tourists, who have high expectations indeed when it comes to Greek food and drink.

However, before you settle down for a meal, make the 45-minute ascent to the **fortress of Feraklos**, enthroned on the hill above Haraki. To reach the ruins of this Crusader castle built in the 14th century, climb up the steps on the southwest side of the hill. Looking out from the citadel, you will have a superb view over the coast north from Haraki.

At the end of the beach promenade at Haraki is the fish restaurant **Argo**, where you can make your own selection from the morning's catch. Red mullet (*barboúnia*), whitebait (*maríthes*) and prawns (*garíthes*) are all excellent options. Don't forget that the prices quoted on the menu are by weight and not per portion.

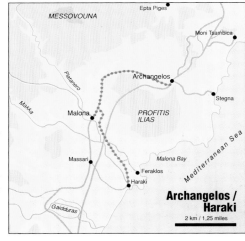

Accommodation

HOTEL KATERINA
45 Rooms, restaurant, swimming pool. Around 15 minutes from the centre, overlooking Archangelos. Tel: (0244) 22169.

HOTEL ANAGROS
26 Rooms. Around 10 minutes from the centre, panoramic view of Archangelos. Tel: (0244) 22248.

HOTEL ROMANTIC
32 Rooms. Quietly situated about 10 minutes from the centre. Tel: (0244) 22185.

HOTEL DIMITRA
Tel: (0244) 22668.

PENSION ANNOULA
10 Rooms. Quietly situated about 5 minutes from the centre.

PENSION NIKOS
11 Rooms. Five minutes from the centre.

PENSION TARALLIS
9 Rooms. Quietly situated about 10 minutes from the centre.

Restaurants

RESTAURANT SAVVAS
On the main street.

PIZZERIA MILANOS
On the main street.

RESTAURANT KANARIS
Just off the main street.

RESTAURANT TASSOS
Just off the main street.

Vehicle Rental

RENT A CAR ANTONIO
Tel: (0244) 22524/22881.

RENT A CAR TSAMPICA
Tel: (0244) 22145. Fax: 22857.

Tourist Information

TSAMPIKA TRAVEL
Tel: (0244) 22145. Fax: 22857.

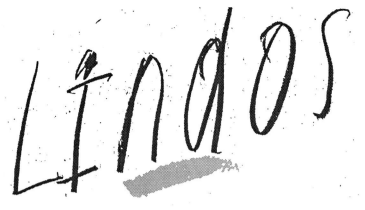

Ancient Lindos

Along with Kamiros and Ialyssos, Lindos was one of Rhodes' three ancient settlements. This once thriving city, whose golden age began with the arrival of the Dorians, sustained itself primarily through seafaring and trade. It prospered due to its favourable, sheltered location on the island's east coast. As a member of the League of Six Cities or the Doric Hexapolis, it administered the entire southeastern segment of the island. By as early as the 7th century AD, tt had a population of 16,000. The city cultivated overseas trade relationships and minted its own coins as well as maintaining such colonies as Sicily, Spain and the Balearics. The pioneering Lindian maritime law was accepted as binding for sea travel in general. Under the 'tyrant' Kleoboulos, one of the seven sages of the ancient world, it developed into a cultural centre of international renown. Two marble tablets, found on the Acropolis, record the roster of ancient VIPs: Herakles, Agamemnon and Helen of Troy, the King of Persia and Alexander the Great.

However, with the Persian Wars, its membership in the Delian League and, not least, with the rapid ascendancy of Rhodes City (founded in 408BC), the metropolis declined in significance. Lindos did not regain its position as an important trading port until the invasion of the Venetians in around AD1200.

52

The Lindian Acropolis

Lindos Today

Nowadays, Lindos is a comparatively small village which in the summer months threatens to burst at the seams with visitors. Half a million tourists a year stream through its narrow alleys. It is considered the island's main attraction, and its historical monuments have been placed under protection as a result. You have to park and walk into the village as traffic is banned.

The golden sands of Lindos Bay are packed and there are all kinds of watersports. By day the village hums with activity in the souvenir shops, bars and fast food places, from burger joints to *crêperies*, and after sun-down there's plenty of night life. There's a new night club and disco with a swimming pool and many of the old sea captains' mansions have been turned into trendy bars.

Accommodation is expensive and scarce. Although there are luxury hotels on the outskirts and a few village pensions, most Lindian houses have been taken over by British companies for self-catering holidays. Information about accommodation is available from the Tourist Police, whose office is in the main square.

Historical Tour of Lindos

Morning tour: an early breakfast at Alexis; ascent, by foot or donkey, to the Lindian Acropolis, with its ancient temple complex and medieval ramparts; a swim, with or without bathing suit, in the Aegean; a stroll by the 'Captains' Houses' of Lindos, followed by a visit to the Panageia Church.

In order to escape the hordes who descend on Lindos during high season, you should wake as early as possible – 8am, at the latest – and head for the **Acropolis**. By setting out early, you will make the rather strenuous ascent in the cool of the morning, and avoid the long queues at the entrance to the site.

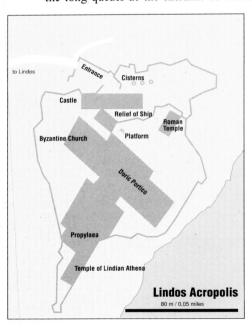

to Lindos
Entrance
Cisterns
Castle
Relief of Ship
Roman Temple
Byzantine Church
Platform
Doric Portico
Propylaea
Temple of Lindian Athena

Lindos Acropolis
80 m / 0.05 miles

Today, modern Lindos is a small town, which managed to retain its village character through the 1960s only to succumb to the influence of tourism in the 1970s. It's not too difficult to find your way round from the central bus stop but otherwise the maze of lanes can be confusing. Follow the main street down to the Church of the Panageia, where the Acropolis is clearly signposted. You might want to grab a quick breakfast at **Alexis** on the way. If you don't want to walk up to the Acropolis you can take a donkey or Lindian taxi from behind the main square where the drivers wait with their donkey trains. Your 'donkey taxi' will take you around the northern inlet to admire the imposing citadel complex from below.

Pedestrians should take the steep stairs which lead up from the village centre through the narrow alleys lined with gift shops, passing the gleaming white facades of the houses with surprise views into their picturesque courtyards. On the edge of the village, the

Lindos' medieval ramparts

main street becomes a dirt path, with steps cut from the stone of the Acropolis itself. Be very careful here. The steps are extremely slippery, worn smooth by the tramp of countless feet over the centuries. If, by chance, you are interested in handmade lace, a local craft, you might want to pause under the cedar trees en route to the citadel, and take a look at the tablecloths offered for sale there by Lindian women.

After inspecting these wares, you will find yourself at the entrance to the **Acropolis**. Purportedly, the site was first occupied by tribes which emigrated here from Asia Minor. They are believed to have first worshipped their mother-deity, **Lindia**, a goddess imported from the East, in a grotto beneath the ancient temple site. Lindian myths later merged with the cult of the goddess **Athena**. The temple erected on the summit in honour of the Greek warrior-goddess is supposed to have been in existence at the time of the Achaians and Dorians. Since then, it has been extensively remodelled, expanded and altered to fit the needs of subsequent generations of inhabitants. What you see today above modern Lindos are the remains of buildings which were reconstructed after a huge fire in the temple in 320BC, as well as a medieval castle which was later integrated into the ancient site. As you enter the site, you will see why the **Grand Masters** built upon the remains of the pre-Christian sanctuary. The site is a natural, strategic

Approach to the citadel

Lush vegetation in the environs of Lindos

stronghold commanding views of both the island's interior as well as the coast.

Next to the wall of the citadel, you can still find the remains of **ancient cisterns** which supplied water to the residents. To the left, in front of the exterior stairs, the right-angled steps of which are part of the Italian renovation, you will find the 5th-century bas relief of an ancient trireme (galley developed as a warship) carved into the rock. The prow of the ship once held a statue of Agisander, priest of Poseidon, who, the inscription tells, was awarded a golden laurel wreath by the Lindians for judging their athletic events.

The magnificence of this site, with its seamless marriage of architectural styles from several epochs, is clearly evident as you emerge from the defensive walls surrounding the medieval command post into the bright, open terrace laid out by the ancients. This was once the location of the **Stoa**, a hall bordered by tall columns, 20 of which have been reconstructed. Unfortunately, much of the site is covered in scaffolding. Among the niches, Doric columns and remains of medieval walls, you will see openings into the ancient system of cisterns before climbing to the upper terrace. Here is where the **Propylaea**, a colonnaded forecourt outside the **sanctuary to Lindian Athena**, was located. The temple at the top of the plateau, encompassed an area about 23m (25yds) long and 8m (9yds) wide. It housed the statue of the goddess, whose official status as patroness of the city of Lindos has been documented as dating from around the 4th century BC. The remains of the Temple of Lindian Athena are perched on the edge of the cliff and from this high vantage point, you have a goddess's-eye-view: to the left, below the Acropoli, is the **Bay of Lindos** with its beaches and, to the south, the **Bay of St Paul**, where the apostle is thought to have sheltered from a storm in AD51.

Take the donkey path down from the Acropolis

Byzantine wall painting in the Panagia Church

for a dip in the Aegean at **Pallas Beach** directly below. If you want to cast your bathing costume to the wind then the nudist beach is a few hundreds metres beyond the sands.

After a dip, it's back to bustling little Lindos town. The tour coaches, which arrive every half hour, will have off-loaded an enormous number of visitors since you set out this morning. This uninterrupted stream makes the main street resemble a pedestrian mall back home. Despite the throng, it's worth stopping to take a closer look at the old houses. Beyond the huge stone walls you'll find the lovely Lindian *archondika,* or seacaptains' mansions, dating from the 15th to 18th centuries. Hidden away behind imposing doorways with embellished stone porticos in all kinds of styles, the houses are built around courtyards full of flowers, decorated with traditional black and white pebble mosaics, or *hoklakia.* Inside, the floors are also studded with pebbles in ancient patterns. The facades of the captains' houses are carved with Byzantine and eastern designs as well as twisted ropes and chains to symbolise the seafaring heritage

Snow white Lindos

of the owners. There are balconies built out over the alleyways as well as special captains' rooms over the doorways which guaranteed views of enemy movements out at sea.

To round off your tour of Lindos, it's worth visiting the little **Panageia Church**, in the centre of the village. This late Byzantine church of the Assumption of the Virgin Mary, or Panagia, was built on the site of a 10th-century basilica and restored by Grand Master Pierre d'Aubusson between 1489–90. The interior walls are almost covered in frescoes painted by Gregory of Symi in 1779 and refurbished in 1927. Watch out for St Christopher depicted with the head of a jackal after he prayed to God to make him less attractive to women. Also worthy of note here are the beautifully laid floors of pebble mosaic (*hoklakia*), which are so typical of the interior courtyards and living areas of the rich Lindians.

For your afternoon meal, try a restaurant on the road to Kalathos. **Panorama**, 3km (2 miles) out of town, serves prawns wrapped in bacon on the skewer, and other delicacies. The restaurant's name is apt, as the site overlooks the Vliha Bay and **Lindos Bay Hotel**.

The Tomb of the Tyrant and Evening in Lindos

An afternoon walk to the tomb of Kleoboulos; dinner at the Xeno-mania Restaurant; a visit to the Qupi bar; and late-night dancing at the Acropolis or Epos discos. Begin in the late afternoon, ideally about two hours before sunset so you will be sitting down to dinner just as the sun begins its slow, summer descent.

From the main square in Lindos, walk down Kleoboulos Street to-wards the beach, then follow the sign right to the restaurant **Xeno-mania**. The route leads through a small olive grove to the attractive open-air restaurant and bar. Behind the restaurant, the path leads out onto a spit of land. Continue straight on, towards the windmill before the **Hill of Kleoboulos**.

Nowr clamber uphill and soon you will find yourself standing before an impressive monument, originally covered by a half-dome roof. According to tradition, this building – which dates from the 1st century BC – is the **Tomb of Kleoboulos**. As 'tyrant', Kleoboulos ruled Lindos for 40 years during the 6th century BC. His tomb – if it is his tomb – was erected several centuries after his death. Con-sidered one of the seven wise men of ancient Greece, Kleoboulos has gone down in history not only as a notable ruler, but also as a poet and philosopher and source of the well known saying: 'Mod-eration in all things'.

From here, you will have a wonderful view of the Bay of Lindos, the white houses of the village and, towering above, the majestic fortress walls of the Acropolis.

Returning back down the hill to **Xenomania**, try to get a table on the edge of the terrace, where you can enjoy the view over the bay. Here you are, sitting in the middle of Lindos, but far removed from the crowds and din which predominate elsewhere. Dine to the strains of classical music or Flamenco guitar. The restaurant attracts discerning clientele.

After dinner, a visit to the **Qupi bar** should round out your evening nicely. Stroll back to the main square and turn into the alley leading uphill to the right just behind the donkey 'taxi stand'. Pass the bars called Sokrates and Lindos by Night. About 50 paces further on you will find the Qupi, whose terrace, decorated with Mediterranean plants, is an inviting place to take a seat. Alternatively go into the bar where you will find yourself in a restored sea captain's house, decorated with mirrors and Greek amphorae (*koupia*), which gave the bar its name.

Those with plenty of stamina left may like to cruise the numerous bars hereabouts, many of them tastefully appointed in old Lindian houses. Afterwards head for the Acropolis disco or the new Epos night spot, just out of town, with its bars, nightclub and swimming pool, open until the early hours.

A Whole Day Adventure Across the Island

From Lindos via Pefkos to Lardos and Laerma; on to Platania and Eleoussa by way of the Founktoukli Monastery; to Profitis Ilias and Embonas, and Taverna Chasapo; up to Kamiros Skala, and the Artemis Restaurant; then back via Siana, Monolithos, Apolakkia, Gennadi and Pilona to Lindos.

From the outset, you should know this is a whirlwind tour, but we will be stopping for breaks, so bring along your bathing costume. A prerequisite is a reliable car – with a full petrol tank – or a sturdy trail bike. The tour will take you right across the island to the west coast, and since we allow minimum time for the return route, you should be able to squeeze in an additional tour to take in sights on the stretch between Siana and Lindos (if you don't want to rush, plan an overnight stay in Embonas or Kamiros Skala). Set out as early as possible so that you will not be driving back in the dark.

Leave Lindos via the car park behind the town, and turn down the narrow road for **Pefkos**. In the morning light, the isolated new hotels look out of place and lost among the barren, rubble covered slopes. However, once you pass the hill beyond Lindos, and get a glimpse of Pefkos, you leave this 'touristic desert' behind, and find yourselves surrounded by luxuriant Rhodian vegetation. Pefkos,

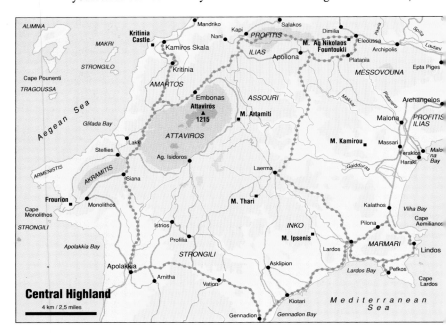

Central Highland

4 km / 2,5 miles

Ruined bridge between Laerma and Apollona

once a rather out-of-the-way settlement in which the donkey drivers of Lindos built their homes, is now a growing resort (it even has a Chinese restaurant and fish and chip shop). There are plenty of bars, and the nightlife is fast catching up with that of Lindos. In the village centre, bear right, continuing in the direction of Lardos until you cross over the large coastal road heading further south. A few metres past this intersection is the turn-off for the village of **Lardos**. The road leads to the centre of town. A series of cafés here – spruced up for the tourist trade – are good places for your first, or second breakfast of the morning (try Anna's Garden). You can count on prices similar to those in Lindos.

Just behind the village square, follow the sign to Laerma, taking the road left and inland. Only a few kilometres out of Lardos is sad evidence of the great forest fire which raged here several years ago. Up to now, all efforts at reforestation have met with little success and although some vegetation is gradually growing back, the charred tree-stumps are a graphic reminder of what can happen if you toss a match or a burning cigarette away carelessly during a rainless summer.

Laerma is in the centre of the island and the village, nestled in the gently rolling hills, has accommodation (used primarily by visitors to the nearby **Thari Monastery**). There are also several authentic tavernas off the tourist trail. Before reaching the village centre head right towards Apollona. After a few metres, the road peters out into a dirt track. Unless you're in a four-wheel drive vehicle take it easy and drive slowly as you could break an axle. It's unlikely you will find help easily should you have an accident in this remote spot. The signs are fewer as the road gets wilder so if in doubt go for the widest road.

After about 9km (6 miles) you will notice a watercourse snaking through eroded stone. Look out for an arch, all that remains of the ruined bridge here. Follow the road that leads towards the water (otherwise, you will end up off to the left in mountains where tree trunks lying across the road make progress impossible). In summer, you can drive right through the little stream here without difficulty. In other seasons, check the depth of water before crossing. Be extremely cautious in winter as flash floods in the area often wash the roads away and people have even been killed.

The wildest part of the route is now behind you. You can now speed up a bit through thinning forest in the direction of **Apollona**. After about 7km (4 miles) you should turn off on the road that leads right towards **Archipolis**. From here, continue via the village of **Platania** to **Eleoussa**, where you should stop in the elegant Italianate square. The crumbling façades and arcades lining one of the long sides of the rectangular plaza belong to the palm-circled governor's palace dating from the time of the Italian occupation. In the years since, the Greek military has taken up residence here, and photography is prohibited.

Finding the way out of town can be puzzling, unless you doggedly

Italianate plaza in Eleoussa

follow the signs for **Mt Profitis Ilias (Prophet Elijah)**, at 800m (3625ft) the third highest mountain on Rhodes. Three kilometres (2 miles) further on you will find the Byzantine chapel of **Aghios Nikolaos Founktoukli** (Saint Nicholas of the Hazelnuts), dating from the 14th century, and remarkable for its magnificent wall paintings. They say that this pretty church got its name from the hazel trees that used to grow on this side of the mountain as *fountoukli* means hazelnut in Greek. There is a magnificent view from the church even if the nut-trees disappeared long ago.

Below the road is a square shaded by plane trees where the former monastery-church celebrated saints' days with feasting and dancing. On Easter Monday, the residents of the surrounding countryside gather for a pilgrimage to visit the **icon of the Virgin Mary of Eleoussa**.

The route continues further uphill through a thickly forested area to Mt Profitis Ilias itself. With each kilometre that you travel, the air grows cooler, and you may even see little wisps of fog clinging to the cliffs. Park in the car park in front of the largest building.

No, this is not some German castle, but instead two impressive hotels, the **Elafos** and **Elfina** (in English, *stag* and *doe*, the island's mascots, which are duplicated on countless T-shirts and figurines). Built in the alpine style by the diligent Italians, in the last few years they have been renovated from the ground up. The hotels now offer category A accommodation, but are open only during high season. After a glance round the game preserve beneath the Elafos Hotel, it is recommended that you drive further on and avoid catching cold.

A short distance uphill the road leads, in seemingly endless serpentine curves, to the other side of the mountain and downhill. At the foot of the mountain, a sign to the left points the way to

Alpine style hotels, Mt Profitis Ilias

Embonas. As well as being famous as the island's premier wine-producing village, Embonas is known for its dancing, particularly by women, and some of the older people still wear local costume as a matter of course. These days the village is a popular venue for Greek nights organised by travel agencies in Rhodes Town. Entertainment is accompanied by copious amounts of wine produced by the village. Then, with a bit of encouragement from the Greeks dressed in their traditional costumes, you can dance the irresistible *sirtáki*. However, for the real thing visit the village at festival time in August, when you'll be in for a treat.

Also in Embonas, knitted, woven and lace wares are sold by local women. If you want to eat here, the **Taverna Hasapo**, a restaurant-*cum*-butcher shop, is recommended. It's next to the modern main church. While you're here, don't pass up the opportunity to try the **local wine** from the barrel or *Suma,* the Rhodian firewater, rather like schnapps. You can have your bottle filled almost anywhere.

Those who prefer seafood to meat should hop back into the car and drive on another 12km (7 miles) to **Kamiros Skala** on the west coast. If you are not too hungry, turn left into **Kritinia**, founded by the Cretans in around 1500BC and today one of the most atmospheric villages on the island.

From Kritinia, as well as from the main road, you can catch a glimpse of the ramparts of **Kritinia Castle** on the rugged west coast. Located exactly halfway between Kamiros Skala and Kritinia, it offers impressive views inland and of the west coast.

In Kamiros Skala, you will be amply rewarded for your long trek at the **Artemis Restaurant**, to the right of the car park area. At any rate, you will be arriving in the little fishing bay with its

Restaurant Artemis in Kamiros Skala

three restaurants well after the midday rush hour, when the place is flooded with hungry passengers from the tourist buses. Have the waiters show you their wide selection of fresh fish and seafood, including giant prawns and lobsters, which are especially recommended, as is the *kalamari*. In comparison to other restaurants on the island, the prices in Kamiros Skala are quite reasonable and may inspire you to return. Your schedule will allow you to stop here for a leisurely lunch.

Your return route, primarily by way of asphalted roads via **Siana** and **Monolithos** to **Apolakkia**, proceeds, straight across the interior to **Gennadion**, with all sorts of interesting intermediary stops along the way (for details of these, see Tour 11: *A Day-long Tour Across Southern Rhodes*). And if you are feeling hot and dusty, you may want to stop off for a swim at the small shingle beach of Fourni, near Monolithos.

Accommodation

Visitors in the high season should expect to find Lindos booked solid by British and Italian tourists. In August it is almost impossible to get a room. Booking in advance through an agency is recommended.

VILLAGE HOLIDAYS
Tel: (0244) 31486

LINDOS SUNTOURS
Tel: (0244) 31333
Rents villas and studios.

To find out about rooms in private homes, ask a local Lindian or stop by the Pallas Travel office, on the main street, tel: (0244) 31494.

Restaurants

In Lindos, as on Mykonos and Santorini, few people use street names when supplying directions. As the village is small and compact, it isn't difficult to find restaurants and bars. Simply keep asking.

MAVRIKO'S
Outstanding restaurant off the main taxi square.

AGOSTINO'S
Romantic roof garden, tasty grill and Embonas wine by the carafe.

XENOMANIA
International cuisine with bar service. From the main square, proceed towards the beach, then turn left at the curve.

HERMES
Refined Greek cuisine; outstanding steaks. Below the Alexis Bar.

SYMPOSION
Traditional Greek food. Located right before the Yannis Bar, across from the supermarket.

PANORAMA
Greek cuisine with an international flavour. About 2km (1 mile) outside Lindos in the direction of Kalathos.

SPITAKI
In the nearby village of Pefkos. Traditional. Excellent seafood.

BUTCHER'S GRILL
Also in Pefkos. Run by family butchers from Lardos. The place for carnivores.

Bars and Nightlife

EPOS CLUB
Fabulous new club for 1,000 people. Includes a swimming pool.

XENOMANIA
For directions to this lively bar see opposite. Open until about 2am.

STAR BAR
Attractive courtyard bar.

JODY'S FLAT
Bar and nightclub, with regular film screenings.

THE LINDIAN HOUSE
In a restored captain's house.

REMEJJOS POOL AND BAR
Stylish place to play biliards.

QUPI
Right in front of the post office. Open until 3am.

YANNIS BAR
Popular hangout in the centre of the village. Good for breakfast.

Money Matters

For best available rates, exchange foreign currency at one of the two banks in Lindos. Don't forget to take your passport, be prepared for long queues, and check the daily exchange rates.

COMMERCIAL BANK
Located in the main town square.
NATIONAL BANK OF GREECE
Located in the area of the bakery.
Banking Hours: Monday to Friday, 9am–2pm, and 5–9pm; Saturday, 9am–noon.

PALLAS TRAVEL EXCHANGE OFFICE
Located on the main street. Business hours: 9am–1pm, and 5–9pm.

Post

The Post Office in Lindos is located near the donkey stand. The service is reasonable and efficient. Hours: Monday to Friday, 8am–1pm.

Telephone

The telephone exchange (OTE) is located by the Alexis Bar on the left side of the street. Hours: Monday to Friday, 8am–3pm. During high season, it is also open at weekends from 9am–noon. Telegrams may also be sent from here.

Medical Care

The ambulance station which also offers first aid is left of the Panageia Church. Hours: Monday to Saturday, 8am–12.30pm, and 5–7pm; Sunday, 10am–noon.

The pharmacy is located next to the post office. Business hours: Monday to Saturday, 9.30am–1.30 pm, and 5.30pm–9pm; Sunday, 10am–1pm.

Transportation

Every half hour, public buses travel between Lindos and Rhodes Town. The central bus station is in the main square. It is best to enquire about daily departures/arrivals and the cost of fares on the spot.

The central taxi stand is also in the main square. If you plan to use a taxi after 7pm, it is advisable to make arrangements ahead of time with a driver.

Shopping

Business hours: Monday to Saturday, 8am–9pm. Sunday, 9am–1pm. Souvenir shops are open all day Sunday. The bakery is open Monday to Saturday from 7am–3pm. It is closed Sunday.

Note: credit cards and traveller's cheques are now accepted by many shops on the island, but if you want to drive down the price of your purchases it is best to offer payment in cash.

Gennadion

This once rather sleepy village was discovered several years ago by northern European travel agencies. This has led to a drastic upswing in tourism in the area and the construction of good pensions and hotels in **Gennadion** itself.

The ample sand and gravel beach features several restaurants in addition to sun umbrellas and beach chairs. The once quaint and quintessentially Greek village shops have given way to modern, self-service stores in which you will now find a selection of German and British beers alongside the rusks and pulses.

Tour 11

A Day-long Tour Across Southern Rhodes

Gennadion, and breakfast at the Village Café; Lahania; Messanagros; The Skiadi Monastery and its miraculous icons; a swim en route to Apolakkia; a visit to a Crusader fortress at Monolithos; Siana; Apolakkia; Vation; then return to Gennadion.

The best place for a bountiful breakfast is the terrace of the **Village Café**. This popular spot is owned and run by a Greek man and his English wife, and they serve practically anything you could ever dream of for breakfast. On the coastal road, drive roughly 9km (6 miles) right from Gennadion in the direction of Kattavia, until you reach a fork for **Lahania**. Here turn away from the sea and

follow the road until you reach a sign for the village. An arrow to the left shows the way to **Café Platanos**, where the narrow, bumpy road comes to an end. Park the car about 50m (55yds) away from the village square – really a circle – with a gigantic, shady plane tree in the middle. This square, in contrast to those of other Greek villages, is not located in the heart of town, but instead at one end. The village church, the Café Platanos and the two fountains make a picturesque composition.

Since the 1970s, a great number of foreigners have settled in Lahania, buying and restoring the dilapidated houses of this village which once boasted a population of 600. In the 17th century, the village was a notorious pirates' lair.

The village population has now shrunk to about 80 Greek inhabitants and some 50 foreign residents, most of whom hail from Berlin and Munich. Unfortunately, the vintage Greek houses are rented primarily to friends of the owners, so a traveller stranded in Lahania will have to seek accommodation in one of the rather scarce private rooms. (Enquire at the Café Platanos or **Chrissie's Coffee Shop** on the upper main street for further information.) The situation should improve shortly with the

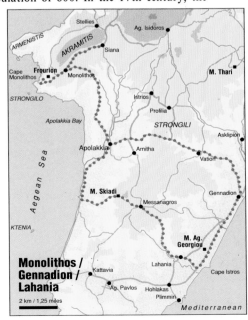

The Crusader fortress above Monolithos

opening of a new pension. A stroll through the narrow, somewhat tortuous alleys of Lahania is worthwhile if only because they are impassable to wheeled traffic. In addition, in the **Lahania Gallery** above the Platanos you can buy ceramics, jewellery, clothing and leather goods, all with a touch of local character and just right for gifts.

Now drive back to the upper village street, turning left there, passing the *kafeneía*, and exiting Lahania on the other side. Just as you put the serpentine stretch up the mountain behind you, follow a road sign to the right towards Messanagros. The well cared for road then turns uphill again, through an area of luxuriant vegetation. After about 10km (6 miles), we see the first white houses of this mountain village, where the **chapel** on the outskirts of town is worth a quick visit.

The old-fashioned mountain village of **Messanagros**, with about 450 inhabitants, was already settled in the 5th century BC. The remains of a small temple here date from this time. On this same site, in years following, an early Christian church was erected. Part of its mosaic, in front of the 15th-century chapel, is still visible. Unfortunately, the rest of the mosaic lies buried under the village road. If you want to view the **Church of the Dormition of the Virgin** – the baptismal font and frescoes are worth seeing – you must find Mike, the proprietor of **Mike's Café Bar**, situated next to the village entrance, and get him to unlock the door for you. However, don't forget to leave a few hundred drachmas behind for the upkeep of the church.

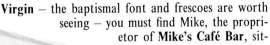

At the edge of the village, we turn left in the direction of

Kattavia, and look for an obscure road sign for **Moni Skiadi** after 1–2km (½–1 mile). The roads are very rough here and a four-wheel drive vehicle is preferable. Head right along a donkey track uphill for about 1.5km (1 mile). Then, switchback curves lead downhill – take this section of the route slowly. About 1km (⅗ mile) further, you will see the idyllic **Skiadi Monastery**, where you will probably be greeted as if you were a long lost friend. The caretakers are always ready to receive visitors, including overnight guests.

The well-kept grounds, with their buildings dating from the 18th and 19th centuries, sprang up around a Church of the Holy Cross which was erected in the 13th century, then enlarged with a broad nave in the 19th century. The church is famous for its icon of the Panagia or Madonna and Child, said to weep tears of blood on its nameday. Legend has it that a 15th-century heretic stabbed the Virgin's cheek, blood flowed from the canvas and the wound and bloodstains are still visible. Over Easter, the church's icons are carried from village to village until, finally, they come to rest for a whole month on the island of Halki. Also, on 8 September, when the annual church festival of Skiadi takes place, the Panagia icons are reverently worshipped by people streaming in from the surrounding region. Afterwards, there is a celebration with live music and dancing, which lasts all night.

Before setting off on the next leg of your trip, to the sea and Apolakkia, enjoy the wonderful view of the **Koukouliari Mountains** and the west coast while sipping Greek coffee at the monastery.

When you reach the connecting road between Kattavia and Apolakkia, turn right and park on one of the paths branching off to the left. Stroll down to the sea for a refreshing swim, but keep in mind that powerful summer breakers produce undercurrents in various places on the west coast. It is advisable not to venture too far out to sea unless you are a really experienced swimmer.

After your swim, it's just a few kilometres to **Apolakkia**, where you should stop in the central *plateía* and have a snack. All four of the tavernas surrounding the square are worth recommending and have kept their prices reasonable.

From the *plateía,* follow the road signs to **Monolithos**, the most important village of the region, some 11km (7 miles) further on through luxuriant green forest. Well on the tourist route these days, the monolith is a 236-m high (774-ft) finger of grey rock with a sheer drop to the sea, topped by a Crusader castle.

From the main street follow the sign for the **Frourion** (fortress). Just 1km (⅗ mile) past the village, you can glimpse the impregnable stronghold, one of the most impressive castle sites in the world. A precarious stairway leads up to it.

The breathtaking view makes the hike worthwhile. It begins in a bend in the road beneath the observation point. Once you have arrived you will find, surrounded by the remains of fortress walls, a little white 15th-century chapel of Ag Panteleimon with interesting frescoes, the arches of the earlier Chapel of Ag Yiorgos, and the foundations of a square building. It doesn't require much imagination to see that here the knights could keep track of all shipping moving towards Crete and North Africa.

To reach **Siana**, you must now cut through Monolithos again,

retracing your tracks, then drive straight on for about 7km (4 miles). Park your car just behind the village church next to the **Café-Bar Manos**, and take a look into this typical village *kafeneíon*, with its enchanting view over the mountainous surrounding landscape. The village is famous for its Suma, the local fiery schnapps, and four varieties of seasonal honey, which are on sale everywhere. Suma, strongest in the autumn, is distilled from wine residues, and although brewed illegally in many places, by a quirk of history Siana is the only village licensed to produce it. Mystical qualities have been ascribed to it. It's strong and lethal, so don't let your driver try it. Siana honey also packs a punch and makes a nice gift. Try the flower honey made in spring, thyme in summer, pine in autumn and heather in winter.

You are now ready to start out on the return route, which first leads back to Monolithos and Apolakkia. On the *plateía*, however, do not turn right towards Kattavia. Instead, go left towards Gennadion. Several kilometres further, turn to the right to Arnitha. Then you must bear left, though the road signs do not indicate this. Proceed uphill and, once you have put the summit of the mountain behind you, you are nearing the village of **Vation**, only 7km (4 miles) from Gennadion.

Vation is worth a little side trip. Allow yourself an *oúzo* on the plane tree-shaded village square in the company of elderly villagers before driving back to Gennadion. Here you can still experience something of the friendly composure of unspoilt rural Greece.

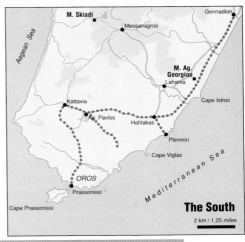

The South

2 km / 1,25 miles

A Day on the Southern Beaches

From Gennadion; sun and swimming at Hawaii Beach; Cape Prassonissi; Greek coffee at Kattavia; a seafood meal at Plimmiri. This tour is dedicated primarily to the pleasures of swimming, sunning and relaxing under the southern sun.

Sleep your fill and then start out from Gennadion in the direction of Kattavia after a generous breakfast at **Klimis**, on the beach. After roughly 16km (10 miles), having passed the point where the road branches off towards Plimmiri, you will notice on the left two avenues which were laid out by the Italians. This was once the settlement of **Aghios Pavlos**, the location of a prison dating from the Italian occupation, which is used today as a pig farm. Turn into the first of the two avenues and drive along the country road towards the sea, till the way peters out in sparsely vegetated sand dunes. Behind the dunes, you will see a broad, sandy beach, usually deserted. If you start out from here and hike to the right along the beach (*not* barefoot), after about 10 minutes you will arrive at the end of the elongated bay, and a spot protected from the wind and shaded by cliffs. Stay here for a wonderful hour or two of swimming, sun and seashell gathering.

The southern tip of Rhodes: Prassonissi

Continuing on from Aghios Pavlos, follow the main road for about 3km (2 miles) in the direction of **Kattavia**Keep to the left at the fork just outside the village. Some 100m/yds further on you will see a road sign for **Prassonissi** (Leek Island), pointing off to the left on a 7km- (4 mile-) long gravel road to the southern tip of the island. This is where west and east coasts meet. The strong wind which blows here most of the time produces strong breakers, attracting experienced surfers.

You will also find two relatively new tavernas serving fresh fish at the narrow isthmus to the little peninsula which stretches out beyond Prassonissi. For the time being, you should deny yourself another ample meal and, instead, depending on the weather (in winter the sandy connecting spit is flooded), take a half-hour stroll to the **lighthouse** on the other side of the peninsula. However, do

Fishing boat in Plimiri bay

not attempt to cover this distance by car since it's quite possible you'll get stuck in the sand. A motorcycle is much more suitable, if your feet are really that tired.

Back at the fork in the main road, you can either turn off to the right towards Plimiri, or drive straight ahead and pay a brief visit to the village of **Kattavia**. After 200m/yds, you will find yourself in the central *plateía*, which is flanked by several *kafeneía*. At the **Café Tofos**, you can take a seat in the shade of an expansive tree and study the languid village life of the residents who have, for the

Church in Plimiri

most part, been spared the ravages of tourism. The only variation in the texture of village life is brought about by the military who are stationed in the area.

Since you are likely to be rather hungry by now, drive 8km (5 miles) back down the main road to the fork for **Plimmiri**, which is at the end of a 1.5km (1 mile) long side street. The outstanding fish restaurant here, **Yannis Galantomos**, and the romantic view over the little fishing bay, on which a longer swimming beach is located, are probably going to detain you a little longer in Plimmiri.

If you walk up to the hills behind the restaurant, you will come across a collection of ruined homes dating from the German occupation. To the right of these, the ancient city of **Kyrbe** is said to have stood. However, it fell victim to a flood (Greek: *plimmiri*), hence the name of the current village lying below. A later village believed to have existed here was called **Ixia**.

The church which is located just behind the restaurant was itself erected atop the foundation walls of a much earlier Christian basilica, whose columns and marble work have been incorporated into the present building. In the front yard of the church is a pond which was once the site of a spring said to have miraculous powers.

A Motorcycle Tour of the Southern Coast

A half-day tour from Gennadion; to Kiotari; Asklipion; the Thari Monastery; Laerma; and Lardos.

We will be leaving the village of **Gennadion** on the coast road heading north. Pass a petrol station and continue on to the intersection for **Asklipion** (left) and **Kiotari** (right). Bearing right, you will find a beach as beautiful as the one at Haraki. Pull off the road and take a swim. Although many well situated restaurants can be found here, Stefanos (on the left) serves the best fish. Ask

Laerma / Asklipion / Lardos
4 km / 2,5 miles

to see the day's catch, and remember that Rhodes is famous for its red mullet, swordfish and lobster.

Stay on the coast road for **Asklipion**, where the oldest church on the island draws many Greek tourists. The Byzantine **church of the Dormition of the Virgin** was built in 1060 and has some fine 17th-century frescoes. If it is closed, ask at the *kafeneion* for the key.

Named after Asklepios, God of healing, the village stands on the site of the island's ancient medical centre and even now the sick come to pray for healing at the church. It's a fascinating village and many people still bake their bread in communal ovens in the street.

The ruins of a medieval fortress, known locally as **Iannis Castle**, brood above the village, one of the most southerly strongholds of the knights. The walk up takes about 15-minutes: just follow the track from the public toilets.

Leave the village via one of the upper streets, and head northwest for about 7km (4 miles) via the road for **Laerma** and **Moni Thari (Thari Monastery)**. This will take you diagonally through a forest. Two kilometres (about 1 mile) before you reach Laerma, is one of the island's most precious treasures. Legend has it that a Byzantine princess, afflicted with a fatal illness, had this monastery built so that she might retreat to the wilderness and there die in peace. The monastery was duly built, and the princess miraculously recovered.

The picturesque monastery buildings were most probably erected between the 9th and 13th centuries, although the foundations date from before the Christian era. Thari is famous for its frescoes. Some walls have four layers of paintings spanning the 12th–18th centuries and the apse has especially fine paintings dating from the 12th–16th centuries. Look out for the apostles in shades of red ochre, black and cream, and on the right wall the head of a dappled horse, probably part of a painting of St George.

A huge annual festival is held here every June. Thousands of people from all over Rhodes and elsewhere gather here to feast and dance the night away. From the monastery, proceed in the direction of **Laerma**, where several *kafeneía* will tempt you in for a refreshing pause. Try a Greek 'spoon sweet', *glikó koutalioú*, with your coffee. Continue on towards **Lardos**. Ask for directions to the workshop of Lynn Fischer, whose ceramics represent a departure from most ware to be found on Rhodes.

Tourist Information

PALLAS TRAVEL
Tel: (0244) 43340. Hours: Monday to Saturday, 9am–1pm; 5–8:30pm. Best travel agency in Gennadion.

Accommodation

TINA'S APARTMENTS
For information, contact Pallas Travel.
BETTY STUDIOS AND APARTMENTS
In the centre of town.
IRENE'S PENSION
In the centre of town.
DENNIS BEACH STUDIOS
Located outside the town centre on the beach; contact Pallas Travel.
KIOTARI VIEW
Tel: (0244) 43349).

Restaurants

KLIMIS
Beach location, with an attractive terrace, and reasonable prices for quite good food.
ANTONIS
Also on the beach, with a beautiful terrace, and outstanding food. Tel: (0244) 43300.
ST GEORGE
Situated about 1km (⅝mile) past Gennadi on the coastal road towards Kattavia. Tel: (0244) 43267.

ROBERT'S
Located in the main street, British ambience.
EL GRECO
Between OTE (the telephone exchange) and the Post Office.
THE THREE BROTHERS
On the coast road.

Cafés and Bars

CAFÉ MEMORIES
Next to the supermarket.
VILLAGE CAFÉ
On the main street.

Vehicle Rental

KOALA RENT-A-CAR
Right at the entrance to the village. Tel: (0244) 43304.
TEO RENT-A-CAR
Lahania, reasonable rates. Tel: (0244) 43390.
EXPLORER RENT-A-MOTO
Tel: (0244) 43256.

Medical Station

On the coastal road at the entrance to the village.

International Press

THE THREE MILLS
Located in the village centre. Tel: (0244) 43033.

Dining Experiences

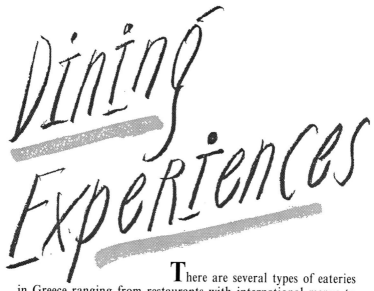

There are several types of eateries in Greece ranging from restaurants with international menus to *psistaria*, tavernas which specialise in roasts and barbecues to order. Tavernas are open for lunch and dinner and usually have an array of ready-cooked oven dishes to choose from, such as *ladera*, vegetables or meat stews in rich olive oil and tomato sauce; *stifado*, a spicy stew of beef or rabbit; *moussaka*, layers of aubergine with potato and minced lamb topped with bechamel sauce; and *pastitisio*, Greek lasagna. They may also offer pork cutlets, roast lamb and *souvlaki*, kebabs of pork, chicken or lamb on a skewer. Roast chicken is usually delicious and often free-range.

Vegetarians are reasonably well served with *gigantes*, giant butter beans in tomato sauce; *fasolakia*, green string beans; *briam*, a mix of aubergine, courgette and tomatoes rather like *ratatouille*; *horta*, local greens tossed in oil and lemon; and delicious *tiropittes* or *spanakopittes,* cheese or spinach pies in light *filo* pastry.

Fish appears on the menus in two price categories generally quoted per kilogram, not per portion. The fish favoured by Greeks, and the most expensive, are **barboúnia** (red mullet) and swordfish. Cheaper, though sometimes chewy if frozen, are **kalamária** (fried squid) and grilled octopus. In season, small fish like whitebait, *merida* and *atherina* are cheap and tasty.

In the tourist centres, international cuisine has been introduced, in which pizza and pepper steak are star players. In Rhodes Town, fast food restaurants have sprouted up, crowding out the traditional *gyro* and *souvláki* stands. Also popular are *geletaria,* which sell frozen yogurt and a multitude of ice-creams. The use of microwave ovens has now become so widespread that dishes which were traditionally served at room temperature now burn your tongue.

Rhodes still boasts truly gobal cuisine with Mexican, Cantonese, Indian, French, Italian, Scandinavian and British eating places all competing for custom. Complimenting this versatility, are some exceptional Greek tavernas offering imaginative Greek cuisine and fine international restaurants in the luxury hotels.

Tipping customs are as follows: in addition to the service charge which is included in the price of a meal, a 5–10 percent tip should be left for the waiter. Also, don't forget to leave something for the assistant waiter who brings the bread and clears the dishes and earns little for his pains.

Beverages

On any occasion, as an aperitif, after meals, as well as in between, **oúzo**, a liqueur flavoured with anise, is popular. In the countryside it is drunk undiluted, taken in sips alternating with sips of cold water. In the city, it is often served with ice or mixed with cold water. A little glass of *oúzo* consumed at the appropriate time settles the stomach and calms the mind. In the *kafeneía*, it is usually served by the glass or in a *karafáki*, small carafe. Unfortunately, the custom of serving *mezéthes,* morsels of cucumber and cheese, olives or nuts with *oúzo,* is dying out.

Greek coffee is consumed either *glikó* (sweet), *métrio* (medium) or *skéto* (without sugar). Sugar is not served on the side, but boiled with the coffee. The grounds remain at the bottom of the cup as you drink, and should stay there.

Wine is normally dry, but varieties designated 'demi-sec' are sweet. The wines offered in most restaurants come from the large bottling firms of Caïr and Emery. Caïr distributes the Ilios (white) and Chevalier (red) labels as well as the expensive white, red and rosé Moulin. Emery wines also come in white, red and rosé. Look out for the excellent crisp white Villare and the newer red Mythiko. Tsantali is also recommended. Beyond Caïr and Emery, some table wines worth recommending are the Calliga, Boutari, Nemea and Apelia labels. **Retsína**, or resin flavoured wine, is less than half the price of non-resinated, but it's an acquired taste. **Kourtaki** is an old favourite and comes in flip-top half bottles, but the local CAIR has a more delicate flavour. **Beer** is well on the way to pushing aside wine on the Greek table. Among the beers produced under licence, such as Henninger, Löwenbräu, Amstel and Heineken, the last leads the pack. Greeks generally prefer an icy Amstel.

Shopping

Rhodes has stocked its supermarket shelves to meet the requirements of visitors from the north. In all the larger stores you will find the products you use at home. In Faliraki, the shopkeepers have gone the whole hog and you can now see fake Safeways, ASDA etc shop signs over little local supermarkets, the logos pinched from British carrier bags! Furthermore, there are off licences everywhere, though their prices have rocketed in recent years. Still, purchasing spirits on Rhodes is worth your while, since alcoholic beverages are still around 20–30 percent cheaper than in much of the rest of Europe.

Tobacco products are a similar bargain. A carton of cigarettes manufactured under Greek licence (Marlboro, Camel etc) costs about 40 percent less on Rhodes than in Britain, for example. Even more reasonably priced are domestic cigarettes such as Assos, and the popular Karellias.

Souvenirs

In Rhodes City you will find **jewellery** shops on every corner where distinctive 'Greek gold' designs sell for comparatively reasonable prices. Of course, the art of gold working has a long tradition on Rhodes, though most of the jewellery sold on the island today is produced in Italy.

The Athens based jeweller **Ilias**

Lalaounis maintains a shop on the former Auberge de l'Auvergne, where flawless copies of ancient designs and collections featuring Byzantine elements, rock crystal or pavé diamonds may tempt you.

The **Ministry of Culture** shop on the corner of the Street of the Knights specialises in replicas or artefacts from the museum. The statues, etc are sold with certificates of authentication.

In the city, **leathers and furs** are also offered for sale. This may seem rather peculiar considering the often sweltering heat. One of the best shops is **Dano Niko**, 92 Socratous Street, which also stocks vibrant kilims made in the village of Embonas.

Ceramics, embroidery and woven carpets are also traditional Rhodian products, but the quality is variable.

Hand-painted ceramics can be found at **Phidias**, on Panetou Street. The motifs on this ware are based on ancient patterns

though more modern designs are also available. Equally worthy of mention are **O Myrina**, on Griva Street, where you can also buy ceramic figurines, and the **Greek Gallery**, 74 Socratous Street. Rhodian ceramics it should be noted, are famous throughout Greece. Traditional designs are outlined in black on a white or cream background, then hand-painted in bold colours. Lamps and huge platters will add stunning accents to monochrome rooms back home. Located in the area of Archangelos is the **pottery workshop** of **Panagiotis**, who produces amphorae in the old style, pots and bowls, and other ware. His ceramics are unpainted for the most part, but the simple, pleasing shapes of his everyday articles are decoration enough. Right on the main road as you enter the village of Archangelos is the **Neofitou Ceramic Manufactory**, where you can obtain fine copies of ancient ceramics.

You can purchase **handmade lace** most reasonably in Lindos, where this art has long been practised. In Archangelos and Afantou, you can buy beautifully made woven **carpets and runners** at remarkably low prices, as well as handmade traditional **boots**. In Siana, a small mountain village on the west coast, you can obtain superior quality **honey** and **soúma**, a homemade grape spirit which comes close in taste to Italian *grappa*. You can buy **wine** in bulk at Embonas. Also located here is the largest wine company in the region, Emery.

PRACTICAL information

Travel Essentials

Travel To and From Rhodes

The most comfortable way to reach Rhodes is by air. Although you can never be sure that the airport bank will be open upon your arrival, you can exchange money at any time, at a reasonable rate of exchange, at the Olympic counter. It is here, too, that tickets for the bus transfer to Rhodes City are sold.

The Olympic Airways Bus, which runs to complement Olympic Airways arrivals/departures is the most comfortable and economical way to get to the new city (16km/10 miles away). It goes directly to the Olympic Airways City Office, which is centrally located.

In addition, there is a regularly scheduled public bus for Rhodes City which stops outside the airport.

A taxi from the airport into Rhodes Town costs roughly 3,000 drachma depending on the time of day and the amount of luggage you have. If another passenger turns up going the same way as you, do not be surprised when the taxi driver charges you both the full fare. In Greece this is 'legal', if not the letter of the law.

If you arrive by ferry, it's just a short walk into the Old Town, but this can be difficult if you have heavy bags. There are plenty of taxis from here into the New Town, but if you plan to stay in the medieval city note that many taxi drivers will refuse to take you in because the streets are so narrow. It's safer to arrange for your hotelier to meet you or invest in a folding luggage trolley.

Customs and Duties

All articles for personal use may be brought into Greece duty free. If there is any doubt as to the strictly personal use of an item – a typewriter, for example, a television or video recorder – you may have it entered in your passport so that when you depart it can be ascertained that you are 'exporting' the item with you.

For goods from the duty free shop, there are the following free limits: 200 cigarettes, 1 litre of spirits and 2 litres of wine.

For goods on which duty has been paid in another EU country, limits are considerably more generous.

Changes in Booking

Changes in booking for charter flight ticket holders can be taken care of in most cases without difficulty by the individual carriers' agents in Rhodes City. A prerequisite for changing your ticket is the availability of a corresponding seat on another aircraft. Naturally, you must pay the telex costs and re-booking fees, which vary from case to case.

If your efforts to re-book prove fruitless and it is a case of emergency or illness, you can try to re-book your flight at your carrier's airport check-in counter. If there is a seat available on one of your carrier's aircraft (due to a no-show, perhaps), then the airport manager will probably give you permission to leave without changing your ticket, upon the presentation of a legal affidavit stating the nature of your problem.

Money Matters

Banks

Hours: Monday to Thursday 8am–2pm; Friday 8am–1.30pm. All travel agencies, car hire offices, hotel receptions and most retail outlets can exchange currency and are open virtually all day.

Currency

The Greek monetary unit is the drachma. There are 50 and 100 drachma coins (the 5, 10, and 20 drachma silver coins are rapidly becoming obsolete — most supermarkets or shops tend to round up or down to the nearest 50 or 100 drachma). Banknotes are in denominations of 500, 1,000, 5,000 and 10,000 drachma.

Climate and Geography

Time Zones

Greek time (EMT) is two hours ahead of Greenwich Mean Time. Greek summer time is EMT plus one hour.

Air Temperatures

On Rhodes, summer does not arrive until May, when an average of 25°C (77°F) prevails. June, at almost 30°C (86°F), is considerably hotter, but August, when the mercury reaches a high of around 33°C (91°F), is blistering. Visitors should bring sunblock, and

wear hats and long sleeves to avoid dangerous burns even in spring.

In September, June temperatures return, and October temperatures are similar to those of May. January and February, when the temperature averages around 16°C (61°F), are easily the coldest months of the year. Statistics for the island record peak temperatures of over 40°C (104°F) and lows of nearly freezing.

Sea Temperatures

You will rarely see a Greek in the sea before the beginning of June, in other words not until the water temperature reaches about 21°C (70°F). Tourists arriving from cooler countries are not so sensitive: they jump into the water in May, when the water temperature is 19°C (66°F). By August the water has warmed to about 25°C (77°F), so a dip in the sea is no longer bracing. In October, the temperature sinks again to about 22°C (72°F) and reaches the lowest levels of the year in February and March: 16°C (61°F).

Wind

When the weather is hot, from May till September, the wind known as the *meltémi* blows in from the north to cool brows and tempers. It blows primarily between morning and sunset, and can reach a wind strength of 5 or 6 on the Beaufort Scale. If it reaches 7 or more it will disrupt hydrofoil and ferry schedules as by law the port police are supposed to prohibit all shipping from leaving port for safety reasons. At its strongest it can whisk glasses and bottles off taverna tables and even send chairs hurtling. However, on the whole, visitors are grateful for the cooling effects of this summer breeze. The west coast is particularly exposed, hence

the serried ranks of umbrellas acting as windbreaks on the beaches.

In antiquity, Aeolos, the son of the sea god Poseidon, was considered the creator of the *meltémi*. Today, it is known that strong air pressure gradients between the western and eastern Mediterranean produce these vigorous air movements.

Rainfall

From the beginning of June until the end of August you can be sure that not one drop of rain will fall on Rhodes, even if you occasionally wish one would. April and May average about three rainy days, whereas October averages about six.

In December and January you will need real rainwear. With about 18 rainy days per month, there's little chance of getting a decent tan.

Forest Fires

It is a sad fact of everyday life on the island that each and every summer there will be small, and larger, field and forest fires. However, several years ago almost one-quarter of the forest area of Rhodes was destroyed by a huge fire that cut right across the island. Tragically, the cause of the fire has never been determined. Although even a splinter of glass lying in the right place can cause a fire if the sun hits it at the correct angle, the most common causes of forest fires are carelessness and arson. The fire watch, which was instituted after the great island fire, is designed to spot and fight potential forest fires. The fire watch 'brigade' is spread over the entire island and members are in constant radio contact so that trucks and planes can be called in immediately to douse the flames. Once a fire has occurred, however, the damage is usually irreparable. As a result, the erosion of the island's soil escalates, promoting catastrophic flooding, such as the village of Lardos has experienced since the great forest fire. Greek environmental activists have contributed much through private initiatives and voluntary labourto the reforestation of a portion of the burned woodland.

When camping and walking, holidaymakers should exercise the greatest possible caution to avoid causing fires.

Getting Around

Ferry Connections

Regular ferries operate to other islands in the Dodecanese group and the Aegean, Piraeus, Thessaloniki, Limassol, Haifa, Alexandria and

Marmaris. Details and reservations from all travel agencies or from the following shipping lines:

1. DANE, Odos Amerikis 95, tel: 77070.
2. Red Sea Travel, Odos Theodorakis 13, tel: 27721.
3. Kydon Shipping Agency, tel: 23800.
4. Kouros Travel, tel: 24377, 76178.

There are also day-cruises to Lindos and the south of the island, Symi, Kos and Marmaris. For further information contact the City of Rhodes Tourist Information Centre, Mandraki, tel: 35945, open daily 9am–8pm.

Turkey

If you fly to Rhodes on a direct charter flight via Athens, with no intermediate stop, you may not be permitted to visit Turkey (only a few hours journey by ship from Rhodes) for longer than 24 hours. Other travellers – those who come to the island by ship or scheduled air carrier – are not subject to such restrictions.

Those who are planning to travel in Turkey for longer than 24 hours must present their passports 24 hours ahead of departure time in the travel office. On returning to Rhodes, expect to meet vigorous customs checks.

Taxis

The central taxi stand in Rhodes City is on the Plateia Rimini in Mandraki. To order a taxi by phone, telephone 27666 (this number serves the entire island). Within the limits of Rhodes City, you pay the basic fare. Double fares apply outside the capital.

Bus Connections

Rhodes has a well developed bus network which connects all villages with Rhodes City. The timetable varies seasonally. The central bus terminal in Rhodes City is in the Nea Agora in Mandraki where bus schedules are posted. For information outside the capital, you can phone 20236. Within Rhodes City, call RODA: 27462.

Vehicle Rental

In Rhodes City, you will find representatives of the big international auto rental firms such as Hertz, Avis and Inter-rent, whose prices for their smallest models (Fiat Cinquecentos and similar) are standardised and currently stand at about 12,000 drachma per day (double this for large saloons or jeeps). Local firms offer their vehicles at substantially cheaper rates, particularly off season when competition between companies is fierce. If you waive a receipt and take the car for several weeks, you can get rates of around 8,000 drachma per day off season. The disadvantages of renting from Greek firms is that their vehicles are often in poor condition, and you are usually barred from using them off paved roads. Check you are fully insured before you set off. Some companies won't cover damage to the underside of the vehicle so if you plan to go on rough tracks beware or hire a 4-wheel drive.

Motorcycles and scooters can be rented in all resorts. Rates start at around £8 ($13) for 50cc. Larger motorbikes, up to 1,100cc, are available from a few companies (try Sky or Rent-a-Harley in Rhodes City). A full motorbike licence is required for vehicles larger that 50cc. A crash helmet (supplied) is compulsory.

Mountain bikes and plain push-bikes can be rented for approximately 1,000 drachmas per day.

Bear in mind that the accident rate involving two-wheeled vehicles is phenomenal on Rhodes, so drive with extreme caution at all times.

Traffic Regulations

Although locals appear to take little notice of many traffic rules, foreigners should follow them as best they can. In the event of an accident, tourists are at an extreme disadvantage because of language difficulties. The speed limit in urban/suburban areas and villages is 50kph (30mph). On main roads 80kph (50mph). The wearing of seat belts is compulsory.

The allowable blood alcohol level is 0.05 percent.Police checks are sporadically carried out and offenders are arrested on the spot, and held until trial before a magistrate, which is usually the next day. Anyone driving with more than 0.05 percent of alcohol in their blood is liable to a minimum two months imprisonment or a very stiff fine, plus court costs.

Fuel

Service stations are found throughout the island. Many close at 7pm and on Sunday and public holidays. The price of petrol is slightly lower than it is in the UK and in some other European countries, but around four times the price in the US.

Diesel fuel costs only about half the European price, since Greek vehicles using diesel fuel are used primarily in agriculture, which is subsidised through cheaper diesel prices.

Lead-free petrol is available at all large filling stations.

Health and Emergencies

Pharmacies / Chemists

Chemists are found on most city streets and in major resort villages. Hours: Monday, Tuesday, Thursday and Friday 8am–1pm and 5–9pm; Wednesday and Saturday, they close at 2pm. Details of night chemists, open on a rota basis, are listed in every pharmacy window (or tel: 107).

Many medicines that are only available under prescription in other European countries are available over the counter in Greece. These include Prozac and antibiotics.

Hospitals

Rhodes General Hospital, Red Cross Street, Rhodes Town.
Ambulance available around the clock.
Tel: 22222/25555
First Aid: 25580. In Rhodes Town: 166

Medical Centres

Faliraki: tel: 85555
Afandou: tel: 51393
Archangelos: tel: 0244 22400
Lindos: tel: 0244 31224
Lardos: tel: 0244 44347
Ialysos: tel: 91444

General Practitioner

John Sotirio
Amerikis 50, tel: 30455

Dentistry

Georgios Papazachariou
Iroon Polytechniou, 32, Rhodes, tel: 24516

Dermatology (and Sexually Transmitted Diseases)

Michael S Savingos
Venetokleon 117, tel: 28391

Eye, Ear, Nose and Throat

Alexander Noulis
D. Themeli 83, tel: 27835

Optometrist-Medical Opthalmist

Martin Kannelakis, Amerikis 42, tel: 27646

Gynaecology

Antony Perides
Clinic: G Efstathiou 11–13, tel: 21601
Private: Tel: 23846

Cardiology

Georgios Georglades, 28th October 37, tel: 36827

Bacteriology and Microbiochemistry

Dora Dimopoulou-Ioakim, Ierou Lochou 14, tel: 20524

Orthopaedics

Nicolaos Tiliakos
Kon. Tsaidari, tel: 27818; private tel: 29433

Ophthalmology

Sotirious Karahalios
Sof. Venizelou 1, tel: 28954
Maria Tandidou
G Efstathiou 8, tel: 23244

Paediatrics

L Loukaides, I. Politechniou 20, tel: 25565

Police

Emergency, tel: 100 or 33333
Tourist Police, tel: 27423
Airport Police, tel: 92998, 28928
Ialyssos, tel: 93333
Archangelos, tel: 0244 22160
Harbour Police, tel: 27634

Consulates

America, US Embassy, 91 Vasilissis Sophias Ave, Athens, tel: 721-2951
Austria, 17, 25 March St, tel: 24757
Belgium, Mediterranean Hotel, Kos 35, tel: 24661
Great Britain, 111 Amerikis St, tel: 27306/27247
Denmark, Ionos Dragoumi 5a, tel: 94488
Finland, Politechniou 11, tel: 35780, fax: 36696
France, Kritis 7–11, tel: 22318, fax: 22435
Germany, Monte Smith/Parodos, Issodou, tel: 63730/29730
The Netherlands, Ialyssos Tours, Diakou 25, tel: 31571/33577
Italy, Ippoton St, Old Town, tel: 27342
Norway, Ierou Lochou 11, tel: 27313
Spain, Theodoraki 13, tel: 22460/22350

Sweden, Amerikis 111, tel: 31822/63663
Turkey, Polltechniou 10, tel: 23362/24603

Post and Communications

Post

Main Post Office
Mandraki, Odos Eleftherias, Rhodes City, tel: 22212. Hours: Monday to Friday 7am–8.30pm.

In addition, postage stamps can be bought at kiosks and stationers.

Telephone

The organisation called OTE (*o-táy*) is responsible for telephone and telegraph services, and has offices in all of the larger towns. You can make calls from blue-coloured booths, which take phone cards (Telecartes) bought from kiosks, shops and the Post Office (currently 1,300 drachmas for 100 units or *monades*). A semi-public telephone is usual in the smaller villages, invariably to be found in a *kafeneion* or store. Here you can telephone at the standard rates. Telephones in bars, restaurants, hotels, etc can charge whatever they wish, and often do.

Dialling internationally is straightforward. First dial the international access code from Greece, which is 00. and then dial the country code: Australia (61); Canada (1); Germany (49); Italy (39); Japan (81); the Netherlands (31); Spain (34); United Kingdom (44); United States (1).

If you're using a US phone credit card, dial the company's access number listed below:
AT&T, tel: 00-800-1311
MCI, tel: 00-800-1211

Area Codes

Athens	01
Thessaloniki	031
Kos, Nissiros, Astipalea	0242
Kalimnos	0243

| Karpathos, Kassos | 0245 |
| Leros, Lipsi, Patmos | 0247 |

Local Codes
Rhodes is divided into three telephone networks: the northern sector of the island, up to Soroni on the west coast and Afantou on the east coast, has area code 0241, which is also used for the islands of Chalki, Kastellorizo, Symi and Tilos. The southwest (including the towns of Embonas, Salakos, Monolithos and Apolakkia), has the area code 0246. The southeast (including Archangelos, Lindos, Lardos, Gennadion and Kataria) has area code 0244.

Radio

Radio ERT 2 broadcasts English language news at 2.25pm daily.

Festivals and Holidays

National Holidays

25 March, Independence Day. On this day in 1821 the revolt against Turkish rule began. The day is celebrated with military and school parades.
28 September, Ohi Day. On this day in 1940 the Greek government defied Mussolini's ultimatum demanding capitulation without resistance. Because of this historic 'no', the day is called Ohi Day.

Religious Festivals

Greek Orthodox Easter is the most important festival of the year. The high point is Easter Mass at midnight on Easter Saturday/Sunday. After the service, people gather for a feast.
23 April, Aghios Georgios, celebrated at Kritinia.
Beginning of June, great monastery festival at Moni Thari.
24 June, Summer Solstice, marked by many island celebrations.
29 June, SS Petros and Pavlos, special festivities at St Paul's Bay at Lindos.
17 July, Aghia Marina, at Paradissi.
20 July, Profitis Ilias, in front of Ilias Church on Mt Profitis Ilias.
27 July 27, Aghios Panteleimonas, at Siana.
29/30 July, Aghios Soulas at St Silas at Soroni with competitive events and donkey races.
6 August, Metamorfosis, at Maritsa.
14-23 August, Panageia Festival at Kremasti.
15 August, Dormition of the Virgin, celebrated throughout Greece.
8 September, Festival of the Holy Virgin at Moni Tsambilca, Moni Skiadi and Embonas.
18 September, Aghios Loukas held at Afantou.

Holiday Surcharges

From Christmas until 6 January, as well as during the Easter period, tavernas, restaurants, and taxi drivers demand a 'gift' (*thóro*). This amounts to about 150 drachma in taxis and 10 percent extra in restaurants).

Photography

In the larger villages colour negative as well as slide film is available. The prices are, however, between one-third and 50 percent higher than in northern Europe and America. It is therefore a good idea to bring sufficient quantities of film along with you, protected in a lead pouch available at photographic supply stores.

Etiquette

Salutations

In Greek cities, as elsewhere in the 'developed' West, people pass on the street without greeting one another. However, in Rhodes' villages, it is esential for visitors to greet the locals if they want to avoid causing offence.

From dawn until about 3pm, one says *Kaliméra* (good day). (*Kaliméra sas* is the polite/plural form.) Until nightfall, upon arriving, and until about 8pm upon departing, it is customary to say *Kalispéra* (*Kalispéra sas*). On the other hand, one would say *Kaliníkta* upon arriving after midnight and on departure after 8pm.

If all this is too complicated to master, simply say *Yássou* (familiar/singular form) or *Yássas* (polite/plural form). See *The Greek Language*, page 91 for a lengthier introduction to De-

the south, which are usually semi deserted, you can skinny dip with confidence, as long as there are no Greek families in the vicinity who might be easily offended.

You should not visit beach restaurants in bathing costumes, let alone in an even greater state of undress (believe it not this has been known to happen).

Sport

Golf

There is an eight-hole golf course at Afantou which stages the Rodos Open Tournament in October. Information may be obtained by calling 51451 or 51255/6/7.

Sailing

Information on sailing is available at the Rhodes Yacht Club, Rhodes City, Plateia Kountouriou 9, tel: 23287; or, Camper and Nicholson's Yacht Agency, 26 Amerikis Street, tel: 22927/30504/30505.

motic Greek. Master the rudiments, and Rhodian friends will be surprised and pleased.

Nudism

There are no official nudist beaches on Rhodes. Nevertheless, over time topless bathing has prevailed on all the larger beaches, and you need no longer fear being arrested for wearing only the bottom half of your bikini. On beaches in

Tennis

Tennis Club Rhodos, Konstantinou 20, tel: 25705.

In addition, most of the large hotels in Rhodes City have tennis courts which are accessible to the general public.

Underwater Sports

From 1 May through October, the Rhodos Subaqua Centre offers diving courses with professional instruction. You can learn about other services and facilities available from the club (including boat piloting) by telephoning 33654.

Courses are also offered by the official School for Underwater Sport, Koulia, tel: 22296.

Scuba diving is prohibited in Greek waters unless divers are accompanied by diving school instructors.

Diving for archaeological artefacts in the waters off Rhodes is *strictly* forbidden and a punishable offence.

Windsurfing

Larger hotels provide equipment. The west coast at Ixia and Vliha Bay near Lindos offer ideal conditions. Experienced windsurfers like Cape Prassonissi, on the southern tip of the island. Further details from the Tourist Offices.

Riding

Mike's Horses, tel: 21387, open 9am–1pm, and 4pm–8m. The stables are on the road to Ialyssos/Filerimos.

Hunting

Information is provided at the Hunters' Association in the Nea Agora, tel: 21481. A licence is required.

Culture

Theatre

In summer (April to October), a Sound and Light show takes place every evening near the Nea Agora. The show is presented in English, German, Swedish and French. Information about starting times is available at the entrance.

In the Old Town, Greek Folk Dances are presented daily, except Saturday, at 9.15pm in Plateia Poli during summer. Further information: tel: 20157 or 20085.

The current programme of the Rhodian National Theatre is available at the Tourist Information office.

Cinemas

Rhodes City has several cinemas, the addresses and programmes of which are available at the Tourist Office.

Lindos also has a cinema, which is open only in summer.

Museums

In general, the museums on Rhodes are open Tuesday to Sunday from 8.30am–3pm, closed Monday. Admission is free on Sunday.

Since the crush of visitors is heavy, doors may be shut in your face by 2pm. This applies particularly to the Acropolis of Lindos.

Religion

Places of Worship

Roman Catholic churches: Both Santa Maria and San Francisco are open continuously.
Mosques: On Friday evening Muslims meet for prayer in the Suleiman Pasha Mosque on Odos Sokratous.
Jewish Synagogue: The Synagogue

Shalom, near Plateia Evreon, is open continuously.

Snakes

There *are* snakes on Rhodes, but the majority of these are non-poisonous. Vipers are the only snakes whose bite can be dangerous, but snake bite can be treated immediately at any medical station. Viper bites are unusual since the snakes tend to slip away at the slightest vibration of approaching feet. In May and June you may also encounter snakes in the villages, since they like to lay their eggs where there is masonry and this is the time for renovations. This is no reason to nurture exaggerated fears, as snakes are afraid of people.

Toilets

On occasion, the hygienic standard of Rhodian plumbing leaves much to be desired, although the traditional, Turkish-style squat-toilet has been replaced almost everywhere by Western fixtures. (There's a lot to be said – by physicians – for the former system, but this is not the place to elaborate.) Since there is no mains drainage on Rhodes, toilet paper (and all other paper waste) should be thrown into the bin provided. Sometimes, tourists complain that these pails are overflowing, but if you consider the difficulty of waste disposal and the numbers of visitors who descend on the island in summer, perhaps you will be a little more understanding.

The Greek Language

Greek is a phonetic language. There are some combinations of vowels and consonants which customarily stand for certain sounds, and some slight pronunciation changes determined by what letter follows, but generally, sounds are pronounced as they are written, without additions or omissions. Thus, learning the phonetic values of the Greek alphabet, and then reading, say, street sounds out loud, is a good method of getting the feel of the language. Most Rhodians have some knowledge of English, and most Greeks are delighted to find a visitor making stabs at speaking Greek. Whatever you can accomplish, guide book in hand, will be rewarded.

In addition to pronouncing each letter, you should remember that stress plays an important role in Modern Greek. When you learn a Greek word, learn where the stress falls at the same time. Each Greek word has a single stress (marked in the following vocabulary list with an accent). Greek is an inflected language as well, and noun and adjective endings change according to gender, number and case. Case endings, the rules governing them, and the conjugation of Greek verbs, are beyond the scope of a guide. (For visitors staying on for longer, there are language classes at the Hellenic American Union and other teaching centres in Athens.

The Greek Alphabet

CAP.	L.C.	VALUE	NAME
Α	α	a in father	alfa
Β	β	v in visa	vita
Γ	γ		ghama
		gh before consonants and a, o and oo; y before e, as in year	
Δ	δ	th in then	thelta
Ε	ε	e in let	epsilon
Ζ	ζ	z in zebra	zita
Η	η	e in keep	ita
Θ	θ	th in theory	thita
Ι	ι	e in keep	yota
Κ	κ	k in king	kapa
Λ	l	l in million	lamda
Μ	μ	m in mouse	mi
Ν	ν	n in no	ni
Ξ	ξ	ks in jacks	ksi
Ο	o	o in oh	omikron
Π	π	p in pebble	pi
Ρ	ρ	r in raisin	ro
Σ	σ	s in sun	sigma
Τ	τ	t in trireme	taf
Ε	ε	e in keep	ipsilon
Φ	φ	f in favor	fi
Χ	χ	h in help	hi
Ψ	ψ	ps in copse	psi
Ω	ω	o in oh	omega

Dipthongs

Type	Value
αι	e in let
αυ	av or af in avert or after
ει	e in keep
ευ	ev or ef
οι	e in keep
ου	oo in poor

Double consonants

μπ	b at beginnings of words; mb in the middle of words
ντ	d at beginnings of words; nd in the middle of words
τζ	dz as in adze
γγ, γκ	gh at the beginnings of words; ng in the middle of words

Vocabulary

Pronounce e as in pet; a as in father; i as in keep; o as in oh.

Numbers

one	é-na (neuter)/ é-nas (masc.)/mí-a(fem.)
two	thí-o
three	trí-a (neuter)/tris (masc. and fem.)
four	té-se-ra
five	pén-de
six	ék-si
seven	ep-tá
eight	ok-tó
nine	e-né-a
ten	thé-ka
eleven	én-the-ka
twelve	thó-the-ka
thirteen	the-ka-trí-a/the-ka-trís
fourteen	the-ka-té-se-ra
etc. until twenty.	
twenty	í-ko-si
twenty-one	í-ko-si é-na (neuter and masc.)/ í-ko-si mí-a (fem.)
thirty	tri-án-da
forty	sa-rán-da
fifty	pe-nín-da
sixty	ek-sín-da
seventy	ev-tho-mín-da
eighty	og-thón-da
ninety	e-ne-nín-da
one hundred	e-ka-tó
one hundred and fifty	e-ka-to-pe-nín-da
two hundred	thi-a-kó-si-a (neuter)
three hundred	tri-a-kó-si-a (neuter)
four hundred	te-tra-kó-si-a (neuter)
one thousand	hí-lia (neuter)

Days of the Week

Monday	Thef-té-ra
Tuesday	Trí-ti
Wednesday	Te-tár-ti
Thursday	Pém-pti
Friday	Pa-ras-ke-ví
Saturday	Sá-va-to
Sunday	Ki-ri-a-kí
yesterday	˙kthes

today	sí-me-ra		ticket	i-si-tí-ri-o
tomorrow	á-vri-o		road/street	thró-mos/o-thós
			beach	pa-ra-lí-a
Greetings			sea	thá-la-sa
Hello	yá sas (plural/polite)		church	e-kli-sí-a
	yá sou (sing./familiar)		ancient ruin	ar-hé-a
	ya (abbreviated)		centre	kén-tro
Good day	ká-li mé-ra		square	pla-tí-a
Good evening	ka-li spe-ra			
Good night	káliník-ta		**Hotels**	
How are you?	Ti ká-ne-te?		hotel	kse-no-tho-hí-o

Getting Around
Greetings
Hello yá sas (plural/polite)
   yá sou (sing./familiar)
   ya (abbreviated)
Good day ká-li mé-ra
Good evening ka-li spe-ra
Good night káli ník-ta
How are you?Ti ká-ne-te?
   (plural/polite)
   Ti ká-nis? (singular/
   familiar)
fine (in response)
   ka-lá
pleased to meet you
   há-ri-ka

Getting Around
yes ne
no ó-hi
okay en dák-si
thank you ef-ha-ris-tó
very much pá-ra po-lí
excuse me sig-nó-mi
it doesn't matter
   then bi-rá-zi
it's nothing tí-po-ta
certainly/polite yes
   má-li-sta
Can I..? Bó-ro na..?
When? Pó-te?
Where is..? Pou í-n-e..?
Do you speak English
   mi-lá-te ta an-gli-ka
What time is it?
   Ti ó-ra i-ne?
What time will it leave?
   Ti ó-ra tha fi-gi
I want thé-lo
here/there e-thó/e-kí
near/far kon-dá/ma-kri-á
small/large mi-kró/me-gá-lo
good/bad ka-ló/ka-kó
warm/cold zes-tó/krí-o
bus le-o-for-í-on
boat ka-rá-vi, va-pó-ri
bike/moped po-thí-la-to/
   mo-to-po-thí-la-to

Hotels
hotel kse-no-tho-hí-o
Do you have a room?
   É-hie-te é-na tho-má-
   ti-o?
bed kre-vá-ti
shower with hot water
   douz me zes-tó ne-ró
key kli-thí
entrance í-so-thos
exit ék-so-thos
toilet toua-lé-ta
women's yi-ne-kón
men's án-dron

Shopping
store ma-ga-zí
kiosk pe-ríp-te-ro
open/shut a-nik-tó/klis-tó
post office ta-ki-thro-mí-o
stamp gra-ma-tó-simo
letter grá-ma
envelope fá-ke-lo
telephone ti-lé-fo-no
bank trá-pe-za
marketplace a-go-rá
Have you..? É-hie-te..?
Is there..? É-hi..?
How much does it cost?
   Pó-so ká-ni?
It's (too) expensive
   I-ne (po-lí) a-kri-vó
How much? Pó-so?
How many? Pó-sa?

Emergencies
doctor ya-trós
hospital no-so-ko-mí-o
pharmacy far-ma-kí-o
police as-ti-no-mí-a
station stath-mós

93

Index